PATIENCE

RABBI ZELIG PLISKIN

published by

ARTSCROLL

SHAAR PRESS

Formulas, stories and insights

Published by **SHAAR PRESS**
Distributed by **MESORAH PUBLICATIONS, LTD**.
4401 Second Avenue / Brooklyn, N.Y 11232 / (718) 921-9000

ISBN 10: 1-57819-483-0 / ISBN 13: 978-1-57819-483-4 Paperback

Printed in the United States of America by Noble Book Press

TABLE OF CONTENTS

INTRODUCTION:
THE KEY TO A MAGNIFICENT LIFE

An interview with a highly impatient person paints a compelling picture of why we would be wise to cultivate patience:

Impatience has made me a nervous wreck. I hate to wait. After just a few minutes of waiting, I feel like climbing the walls. My irritation toward others is expressed in my tone of voice and the words that I use. I often regret what I say, but so far that has not slowed me down. My lack of patience has destroyed my marriage. Child-raising has been a long series of disasters for both my children and myself.

Whenever I do something, I feel a need for instant results. I would rather not get involved in projects that need patience. I look on in envy at the accomplishments of people with no greater talents and skills than mine, but who are patient enough to start something that will take time.

I lack the patience to learn new skills. My impatience has caused me to make many decisions that I have regretted. If I had had the patience to gather enough information, I would have saved myself much heartache and regret. I feel that I would need a miracle to become a patient person.

Patience is one key to a magnificent life. It is the foundation for achieving goals. Patience is the willingness to persist and persevere. Patience is needed to learn, to accomplish, to develop our character, and to interact harmoniously with other people.

Chronic impatience destroys one's life. Even milder forms cause considerable pain. Impatience causes stress which is harmful to one's health. Impatience breeds anger, leading to heated arguments and quarrels. Impatience greatly limits what one will learn and accomplish.

The essence of patience is to live in the present. We are impatient because we want to be in the future faster than reality will take us there. Realizing that we are where we are because it's the Almighty's will for us to be there now will enable us to be calm and utilize waiting time more effectively. Since we will generally be in the exact same place whether we will experience patience or impatience, it makes sense to choose to be patient.

"O.K., I've chosen to be patient, but how do I actually become patient?" you might ask. That is what this book intends to answer.

Just as in my other books in this series, the stories are the accounts of many different people I have interviewed or observed over many years.

Patience is a learnable skill. Even those who have been impatient their entire lives can learn to become more patient. Your present resolve and determination will transform you. The formulas, stories, and insights presented here are designed to create patience. It takes patience to master patience. Do yourself a favor and have the patience to read and reread this book. The inner calm you will gain will be a valuable resource in every area of your life.

I wish to express my everlasting gratitude to my parents. The patience of my late father, of blessed memory, and of my mother, may she be well, when I was growing up is appreciated more and more as time passes.

I am profoundly grateful to Rabbi Noah Weinberg, founder and head of Aish Hatorah. His patience to make his vision a reality has had a major impact on the lives of many.

As always I am grateful to Rabbi Kalman Packouz who helps spread the Torah message to many who are new to it.

WHY BE PATIENT?

Why be patient? Observing the life of an impatient person provides the obvious answer. The impatient person himself suffers and he causes distress to others. An impatient person is restless or short tempered, especially when faced with delay or opposition. Impatience creates anxiety and irritation. Others feel uncomfortable around those who are impatient. The haste of the impatient causes avoidable mistakes and errors. An impatient person will say and do many things that are counterproductive.

Patience is the ability to remain calm and serene even when things are not exactly the way you wish. Patience is necessary to get along well with other people. Patience enables you to think clearly before speaking or acting. The more patient you are, the more peaceful and even tempered you will be. Patience makes it easier for you to handle challenges and tests. Patience enables you to remain steadfast despite difficulties, adversity, or opposition.

Patience is a prerequisite for spending adequate time:

...to reach worthwhile goals.

…to integrate the beliefs, attitudes, and patterns to live a joyous life.

…to develop your character and overcome your faults and limitations.

…to learn new skills and gain new talents.

…to make wise decisions.

…to be a successful negotiator.

As you contemplate this trait, you will keep finding more and more reasons why it would be wise for you to master patience.

"You are one of the calmest people I've ever met," I heard someone say to a friend of mine. "Have you always been this way?"

My friend laughed. "If you would have seen me when I was a young child, you wouldn't have said that," he admitted. "I was impatient about everything. I regret the great amount of pain and suffering my impatience caused my parents."

"What's your secret?" that person asked.

"Hard work," my friend replied with a smile. "When I was old enough to realize that impatience would ruin my life, I was totally resolved to become a patient person. I've had a lot of ups and downs. But I knew that unless I made mastery of patience my highest priority, I would suffer and lose out. I still have challenges. I realize that since I began life by being impatient, I need to work harder at being patient than people who are naturally this way. I consider this to be an integral part of my life mission."

LEARN PATIENCE FROM THE IMPATIENT

E very time you see someone who is impatient, you have a heaven-sent opportunity to learn patience. Impatience can look ridiculous. Why is this person so impatient just because something is taking a few seconds longer than he would have wished? At other times, you may look on in revulsion at a parent who is angrily screaming at a young child for moving too slowly. In your eyes this child is moving at an appropriate pace for his age and size. It is the impatient parent who has the problem. When you witness the ugliness of impatience, increase your resolve to master the beauty of patience.

Being on the receiving end of someone else's impatience gives us a firsthand experience of what others experience if we are impatient with them. Doesn't it feel distressful to be rushed by an impatient clerk? Isn't it irritating when someone you call for instructions or to register a complaint is too impatient to hear you out? Isn't it annoying when you are going as fast as you can and someone yells, "Hurry up already!"

Most likely you have an entire mental library of impatient anecdotes and stories. Whenever you recall instances from the past when others have been impatient with you or with someone else, you have a lesson in becoming more patient yourself. From now on each new experience is another addition in your course on patience.

When someone else is impatient, it is easier for us to understand why that person should be more patient. Great! This way we will have many teachers who do not even realize that they are doing us a service by teaching us to become more patient.

I was waiting in line for an overseas flight. Boarding started way in advance of the actual takeoff time. There were two lines. The man right behind me noticed that the other line was moving faster than our line. It was amazing how annoyed he was. He looked totally ridiculous as he was complaining out loud how awful it was that our line was moving so slow while the other line was moving faster. He spoke rudely to everyone within earshot.

I felt like turning around to him and asking him, "Why are you so upset? We're all going to be on the same plane and we have plenty of time left. Enjoy yourself. Don't make yourself and everyone around you miserable!"

I didn't think that he would appreciate this so I kept quiet. Much later when I looked back at that incident, I realized that this is how I must appear to others when I am impatient. That's certainly not how I want to be.

3

THE FIRST PIECE OF WISDOM

What is the very first piece of wisdom cited in *Ethics of the Fathers*? It is to be patient when judging. This speaks volumes for the importance of patience.

A judge who is called upon to render a decision needs to obtain a thorough picture of a situation. The reality of a situation can be very different from what it appeared to be at first. The more information that is gathered, the more likely that an accurate judgment will be reached. This process takes patience.

What is true for judges is true for all of us.

We are all judges when it comes to judging other people in our minds. Before judging someone negatively, ask yourself, "Have I gathered enough data to be certain that my judgment is accurate?" The answer will usually be, "No." Be patient. Don't pass judgment until you have gathered all the relevant information. Even someone who is very patient will not always have enough time and energy to do this sufficiently. Those who lack patience will inevitably make many mistakes.

My teacher, the late Rabbi Chaim Shmulevitz, Dean of Mirrer Yeshivah, used to say that we are all judges when it comes to judging our words and actions. Every time we make a decision we will be having an effect on our future actions and on our present character. This will eventually effect the lives of others. Should I take this action? Should I go there? Should I say what I am about to say? Be patient when making your decisions. Think first. Weigh the data carefully. Your patience in making these judgments is a wise move.

A person who is exemplary regarding being careful about judging others related: "I used to jump to conclusions about the personalities and actions of others. After making a number of serious mistakes, I have learned to be much more patient to gain a broader perspective. Now, when I hear others making judgments without having sufficient evidence, I challenge them, 'How do you know for certain that you are right?' Those who are honest with themselves will acknowledge that they actually are not as certain as they originally sounded."

THAT'S WHAT TIME IS FOR

"**O**ur goal in life is to overcome our negative traits," said the Vilna Gaon. Therefore whenever you utilize your time to transform impatience to patience, you are utilizing your time the way it was meant to be used.

"Time is money" is an often repeated cliché of the impatient. Yes. It might be. But to the wise, time is for character development. Money is external to you. Your character is who you are. It is your essence. Developing your character is more precious than anything money can buy.

Let us take a critical look at these four common statements:

- *"It's wasting my time to repeat myself."*
- *"I don't have enough time to wait for you."*
- *"It takes too much time to work on that fault."*
- *"I don't feel like spending so much time on something that takes so long to see results."*

It is not wasting your time to repeat yourself when the person you are talking to has a real need for the ideas to be repeated.

The time you spend develops your character and that's what time is for.

There are many instances when you are in an actual rush and you do not have time to wait. But when it is just impatience that makes it difficult for you to wait for someone, the time you spend waiting develops your character and that's what time is for.

Working on overcoming your faults is exactly what time is for. If it takes a long time to work on changing a specific fault, the time you spend increases your self-mastery. That's what time is for.

When the results of a project would be an important priority, working on that project is intrinsically precious. As you think long term and develop your character, your use of your time is exactly what time is for.

"My time is too precious to waste" was the quote I was noted for. Did I really not waste time? Of course not. But I was impatient. And it sounds far better to make a claim that time is precious to me rather than acknowledging, "I need you to hurry because I lack patience."

I once delivered my favorite quote to someone much older than me. He smiled and commented, "You are right. Your time is precious. So don't waste it by being impatient with others. Use it to develop your character."

I got the point and have increased my telling this to myself rather than saying it to others.

SELF-IMAGE
OF BEING PATIENT

"It's my nature to be impatient."
"My entire family lacks patience. I guess I lack a patient gene."
"I've always been impatient. That's who I am."

Our self-image molds us. This applies to the strengths we see ourselves as having as well as weaknesses and limitations. Patience is no exception. People who view themselves as being impatient will have hundreds, even many thousands, of reinforcers over the years. For example, if someone became impatient just three times a day for five years, he will have at least five thousand experiences of impatience. Focusing on these experiences will make it relatively easy to be impatient in the future.

By viewing yourself as a person who is patient, you will find it easier to be patient whenever patience is called for. If you have been patient just three times a day for five years, you have at least five thousand experiences of patience. Each new time you are patient adds to your self-image of being patient. Your foundation will continuously become stronger and stronger.

What if someone has a self-image of being impatient? The good news is that this can be changed. One can view oneself as: "I am a person who is becoming more and more patient."

If someone has viewed himself as being impatient in the past it does not doom him into keeping this self-perception for life. Rather, one can say, "I was impatient for 'x' amount of years, and now I am learning the skill of patience." It's never too late to start. You live your entire life in the present. By being patient in the here and now, you upgrade your self-image.

I knew that if I were to view myself as being patient, I would actually become more patient. But who was I going to fool? My reality is that I am frequently impatient. "So this is who I am," I said to myself. I didn't like it. But I felt that I had to call a spade a spade.

I debated this point with someone who tried to convince me that I would gain by viewing myself as patient.

"How can I?" I argued. "I have been impatient so many times."

"But you've also been patient many times, haven't you?" he countered. I had to admit that this was true.

"So you have a right to view yourself as having patience, don't you?"

This made sense to me. Even so, I continued to argue, "But I'm not perfectly patient."

"But you're not perfectly impatient either, are you?"

"I have to admit, I'm not," I said.

"So you have a choice of viewing yourself as an impatient person who is sometimes patient, or as a patient person who is sometimes impatient. The first person to run a four-minute mile didn't do this every day. Yet he probably viewed himself as someone who could do this. Isn't that right? You're better off recognizing the fact that you have been patient many times. This will help you increase your patience in the future."

Fortunately, he was right.

THE ULTIMATE PATIENCE FORMULA

The ultimate formula for mastering patience is: "Make the Almighty's will your will." Those who internalize this will automatically and spontaneously be patient. Repeat this message to yourself over and over again. "I will make the Almighty's will my will."

- "If it's the Almighty's will that I need to wait for someone, that is my will."
- "If it's the Almighty's will that I need to repeat myself, that is my will."
- "If it's the Almighty's will that I need to wait until I find out some information, that is my will."
- "If it's the Almighty's will that something takes much longer than I was hoping it would, that is my will."

You now have a free biofeedback machine that will alert you when you need to increase your acceptance of the Almighty's will. When your body's muscles tighten with impatience, that is a message that you need to increase your level of acceptance. Be grateful for the tension serving as a coach. Express your appreciation to the Creator for giving you this wonderful gift.

If you do not yet feel that you have mastered the skill of accepting the Almighty's will, try doing so for one hour each day. During that hour whenever the Almighty decides that events will turn out differently than you would have wished, say to yourself, "Since this is the Almighty's will, it is now my will." When you experience the benefits of doing this for an hour a day, it will be easier for you to increase the daily amount of time.

I am a strong-willed person and am used to getting my way. As a child my strong will frequently caused my parents to give me what I wanted because I was so persistent. I was a leader in school and eventually became the CEO of a large company.

I was only 40 years old when my physician told me that my heart was the heart of a person twenty-five years older. He told me that I must decrease my stress level or I would not be alive to enjoy the fruits of my success.

I realized that I need to develop a more serene way of being. I had heard many times that the way to do this is to make the Almighty's will my will. Once I was totally resolved to do this, I was no longer obsessed with everything going the way I personally wanted. I was more patient with my family and my employees. I was calm whenever there were delays. Unforeseen occurrences no longer bothered me.

It was now my will that things beyond my control be exactly as they were. I still took action to make things happen and to accomplish. But I now enjoyed life so much more than ever before. I felt an inner peace that I would not have imagined possible for me.

HUMILITY:
THE ROOT OF PATIENCE

Arrogance breeds impatience. The arrogant person is self-centered. When one is afflicted with this vice, one's wants, needs, wishes, and desires are paramount. The wants and needs, feelings and sensitivities of others are ignored. Thinking only about oneself, the arrogant individual is frequently impatient. No one should keep him waiting.

The above describes the extreme: someone with a high level of arrogance. But even those with smaller doses will easily become impatient. What then is the antidote? Humility.

The humble person realizes that everything he is and has is a gift from the Creator. He alone is "dust and ashes." Other people also have intrinsic and infinite worth, for they too are created in the image of the Creator. They, too, have wants, needs, wishes, and desires. This awareness will automatically decrease the level of one's impatience with others.

Humility enables you to realize that you were put on this

earth to fulfill your life mission and so was everyone else. Others are your partners, just as you are theirs. This makes you more sensitive to the thoughts and feelings of others. Internalizing this will give you the essential foundation upon which to build authentic patience. The greater the level of humility, the less one 's need to work specifically on patience. Patience will become an integral ingredient of one's total character.

Attaining humility is a byproduct of our awareness of the awesome power of our immortal Creator. We are finite in the presence of the Infinite. We are extremely limited when compared to the One Who is unlimited. We are minuscule when compared to the immense size of His total creation of which we are aware of only a tiny fraction. And what we are aware of is mind boggling in its complexity, grandeur, and size. Humility is what any intelligent, thinking human will have to experience with even a partial awareness of what has already been revealed to us.

I had assumed that great people who make the most of their lives would be impatient. They have much to do and there is never enough time to do it all. But when I took a comprehensive view of the truly great people I have encountered, I realized that their awareness of the Creator combined with their respect for each person gave them the humility to be more patient than those who accomplished much less.

8

RECOGNIZING YOUR IMPATIENCE

Recognizing your impatience is an important step in mastering the attribute of patience. It is easy to identify the impatience of others. But when we ourselves become impatient, it can happen so automatically and spontaneously that we are not aware of it.

How do you know when you are impatient? Be aware of your patterns. When impatience is strong and intense, we find it easier to detect. Learn your early warning signals. Notice how you speak and what you tend to say when you become impatient. Notice the muscle tension you experience when you become impatient.

Be open to the feedback from others. If someone you interact with suggests that you are impatient, appreciate this opportunity to increase your level of patience. Not everyone who points this out to us will do so in the sensitive and positive manner that we would want. Even so, your strong desire to master patience will enable you to grow and improve from imperfect teachers and coaches.

Whenever you notice someone else's lack of patience, let it remind you to search for your own patterns of impatience. Even if your own impatience is more subtle, you still will benefit by viewing another's impatience as your personal reminder to be more patient.

I would be highly annoyed when people beeped the horn of their cars out of impatience. "Why do they have to be so impatient?" I demanded to know. Since I said this out loud to myself it didn't really have a beneficial effect on any of those drivers.

After one of my stronger reactions, a friend of mine suggested to me, "You can view those horns as personal reminders for you to increase your own level of patience."

I smiled when I heard this. Ever since, I have reframed the horns of cars as a public announcement for me to increase my own level of patience.

I complained to a teacher of mine who kept telling me to remember to be more patient, "I find it difficult to remember to be patient."

"How do you know when it's time to be impatient?" he challenged me.

"It's automatic. I don't consciously try to remember to be impatient. It just happens."

"That's your goal for patience," he said to me. "As you internalize the attitudes conducive for patience, you don't have to remember that it's time for patience. You will be that way automatically."

9

THE LESSON OF IMPATIENCE

We all have a deep and pervasive need for meaning. We want our lives to be meaningful. Not only is this so about our lives in general, but we feel distress and anxiety when we feel that time is being wasted on something that is meaningless.

Impatience teaches us an important lesson. It shows us that our time is valuable and we want to utilize it for meaningful activities.

Time is a precious commodity. It is limited. We do not always remember this. We can easily get into the habit of treating time as if it were limitless. It is highly important to remember that time is valuable. When you become impatient because you feel that someone or something is wasting your time, let it remind you to consistently make the best use of your time.

Some people become impatient after just a minute or two. They can use this reaction as a reminder to ask themselves, "In what ways do I waste my own time?" And then ask, "What are the best uses of my time and how can I arrange to utilize more time on what is truly important in my life?"

Time management has been an issue for me as long as I can remember. If I were asked, "Are you satisfied with the way you are managing your time?" I would have to respond in the negative. In the beginning of the year, I resolved to upgrade my usage of my time. One problem I've often had with resolutions is that I tend to forget them. It was suggested that I utilize feelings of impatience as a reminder to ask myself, "What is the best use of my time right now and in general?" Since then impatience has been a great resource for enhancing my use of my time. I realize that since losing a few minutes bothers me, all the more so I must make the best use of my hours and days.

WHAT ARE YOU SAYING TO YOURSELF?

How do some people create impatience in situations when most people are patient? And how do other people remain patient in situations when most people become impatient? By finding the key factor we will be able to decrease our own impatience and increase our level of patience.

The key ingredient that creates impatience is the pattern of what you say when you talk to yourself. And this is the same ingredient that creates patience. The distinction is what script you are using. There are script patterns that create patience and others that create impatience.

What are some of the scripts that create impatience?
- *"It's awful that things aren't going as fast as I would want."*
- *"I can't stand waiting so long."*
- *"I'm in a big rush right now."*

- *"I'm missing out because things are going so slow."*
- *"I find this distressful and painful."*

What are some of the scripts that create patience?

"Things are going as fast as they are. I will do what I can to speed things up and I will accept the reality with serenity."

"Each second of life is precious. And I won't waste it by causing myself needless distress."

"One never knows where it is best for one to be at any given moment. I will try to make the wisest choices. But I will realize that where I am could be the best thing for me."

"I choose my emotional state and I am committed to living my life experiencing positive, resourceful states."

"Opportunities for personal growth can be found wherever one is and in any given situation. Right now I will look at the present as a gift and an opportunity."

When someone else speaks to you, what they say and how they say it creates energy. Whether this will create positive energy or the opposite is up to that person. And when you speak to yourself, you are the one who chooses whether the energy will be positive or negative. Be totally resolved to consistently create positive energy.

A changing point for me that enabled me to increase my level of patience stands out clearly in my mind. I was waiting patiently for a ride from someone who was to drive several of us to a wedding. We all wanted to be on time, but I felt calm and relaxed. I didn't consider it a problem to arrive later than I would have preferred. But one of the other people waiting kept complaining.

"Why is that person late? We will miss the most important part of the wedding. This is awful. How come he isn't here yet? I should have gone earlier by myself."

I began feeling highly impatient and distressed. Stepping out of the situation, it was easy for me to recognize that this pattern of speech was the source of the distressful feelings I was experiencing.

I saw the distressful effects of being in the midst of a barrage of impatience-causing sentences. "I'm not going to do this to myself," I said with an intense commitment.

DON'T EXAGGERATE

Impatient people tend to exaggerate. And their exaggerating increases their level of impatience. They might say things like:

"This will take forever." (Forever is pretty long, isn't it?)

"I have been waiting for hours." (When the actual time was just fifteen minutes.)

"It's unbelievable how long this is taking." (It's usually believable for those who are aware of how long things take.)

"I could be accomplishing so many great things if this wouldn't be taking so long." (What exactly would they be? We usually imagine that we could accomplish much more than we can actually do in a given amount of time.)

"I'm going totally out of my mind." (Are you really?)

"I've repeated this a million times already." (Exactly how many times?)

When someone exaggerates how long he has been waiting or how awful it is that things are slower than hoped for, it subjectively increases the level of distress.

If you tend to exaggerate, be resolved to look objectively at situations that tend to arouse your impatience. Exactly how long did you have to wait? Know that in the vast majority of instances the situation is not really totally awful and catastrophic.

Those who are masters of patience might even tend to downplay the frustration potential of a situation. Some of the things that they might say are:

"Compared to eternity this waiting isn't very long."

"The environment where I am waiting is actually a rather pleasant place to be. It is actually a paradise if you compare it with the absolutely worst places."

"Repeating something ten times doesn't even come close to the four hundred times Rabbi Praida would repeat each idea to his slow student."

"I'M NOT PATIENT BECAUSE..."

"I'm not patient because my parents weren't patient."
"I'm not patient because of my childhood experiences."
"I'm not patient because I lack a patience gene."
"I'm not patient because of all the stress in my life."
"I'm not patient because I have a deep-seated complex which includes a basic fear of abandonment."

I f someone lacks patience, the way he perceives the root cause is a key factor in how he will approach seeking a solution. Looking at a lack of patience as being rooted in factors over which one has no present control is not the most effective and efficient way to find a solution.

Consider this theory: "I'm not patient because I have not yet mastered this mental skill."

It may be true that someone's parents were not patient, and he had many distressful childhood experiences, and his genes might not have made him spontaneously patient, and he experiences much stress, and he has a complex which includes fear of abandonment. Still, if one has mastery over his brain in the present, he will be patient when the motivation is there.

Many people would find it difficult to watch a super hyperactive child for an entire month. They would say, "I don't have the patience for that." But what if one would be paid a $1million for that month? How many of us would suddenly find the patience? Even those who would otherwise come up with all kinds of reasons and explanations why they lack patience would be able to remain patient for an entire month if that was the condition for receiving payment.

Keep your main focus on mastery of your brain. That is the way to acquire joy, courage, patience, and every other inner resource that will enhance your life.

Focus on your goal of mastering patience. Refrain from building up reasons why you are not patient. Those who keep justifying their lack of patience can very well be successful. They may convince themselves that patience is not for them. But anyone who is serious about the quest for greater mastery over their brain will find themselves improving. Each success breeds greater future success.

As you continue to gain mastery over your brain, you will be able to say, "I am patient because I worked on it."

I spent a lot of time and money figuring out why I wasn't patient. I used to tell my friends, "I'm still not patient. But at least now I know why."

I said this to one person too many. He let me have it. "If I didn't care about you, I would just nod my head and let it go at that. But I do care about you. Stop fooling yourself. You can only master patience when you learn to master your brain. It will take effort, it will take trial and error. But eventually you'll get there as long as you face the right direction."

That did it for me. I was resolved then and there not to build up reasons for not being patient. Rather, I was determined to develop my brain so I could be patient at will.

STEP BACK,
GAIN COMPOSURE

I f you find yourself being impatient, step back and gain composure. When we get caught up in our experience of being impatient, we can forget to step back. We often are not consciously aware that we have become impatient. But as soon as you do become aware, you have the ability to immediately change your state by mentally or physically stepping back.

Imagine another person interrupting your pattern of impatience by screaming at you, "STOP!! HOLD IT!! STEP BACK RIGHT NOW!!!" Imagine that his voice resonated loudly and he shouted this with a powerful, booming blast of his vocal cords. This would shake you out of your state of impatience.

Imagine paying someone to follow you around. This person's mandate would be to shout for you to step back as soon as you became impatient. Just knowing that this person was there would help prevent you from reacting with impatience.

While it is not practical to have a real live person be your constant patience coach, you can create this coach in your mind. Visualize the biggest, strongest most powerful person you can imagine. Mentally visualize him roaring at you, "STOP!! HOLD IT!! STEP BACK RIGHT NOW!!!" You can make this image as large as you want since it is your imagination that is the creative artist.

Your coach is in your brain and you can ask him to pop up as soon as he observes you becoming impatient. Practice visualizing this over and over again. Associate this imagery with the feelings you have when you begin to experience impatience. Keep practicing until you find it impossible to be impatient without this imagery coming to your rescue.

I had what is called, "Low frustration tolerance." This means that I frequently became impatient. I wanted to become more patient, but my impatience was so spontaneous that I didn't know what to do. Someone suggested that I ask the members of my family to say to me, "Step back and access a patient state." I tried this and it worked wonders for me.

MASTERY OF JOY

A master at accessing and creating joyous states will find it easier to master patience. When others stew and fret over delays and the need to wait, they will use the Creator's gift of a brain to experience joyous thoughts and feelings.

People who are frequently impatient need to remember their priorities. Why are they frustrated? Because they want to be someplace or do something and it is not happening the way they want at the speed they want. Realizing that they want what they want in order to experience positive feelings such as joy, they will keep their main focus on joy. This is the end goal. Everything else is just a means to an end.

But not everything we do is for joy. We need to be on time to meet our responsibilities. We need to take care of things for many valid reasons. True. But whenever something is beyond our control at the present, being impatient about it is counter-productive.

How do we master the joy that King Solomon describes as the equivalent of constantly celebrating at a party (*Proverbs*

15:15)? This is the mastery of gratitude to the Creator for all of His gifts. Each breath is a gift. Our sight, hearing, being able to talk and walk are all gifts. The food we eat and the clothes we wear are gifts. Being alive is a gift. Making constant gratitude your reality is the path to joy. And everyone who has ever experienced the distress of impatience will agree that joy is far more preferable.

Whenever you experience the distress of impatience, hear yourself saying, "Choose gratitude and joy right now." Another variation is to immediately ask yourself, "What am I grateful for?"

I like to do things quickly. A few members of my family did things too slowly for my taste. I used to think, "If only they would move faster, I would be much happier."

I tried to rush them, but this didn't help very much. My rushing caused a reverse reaction and things took longer than they would have without the rushing.

Upon the advice of a colleague, I decided to place my main focus on increasing my own level of gratitude and joy. It was amazing how not only did I experience greater happiness, but the family members I tried to rush actually did things more quickly than they had before.

ALERT MIND, RELAXED BODY

The optimal state for learning, understanding, and remembering is the state of: alert mind, relaxed body. When you study in this state, you can become absorbed in what you are reading or hearing. When you are required to take an exam, make a decision, or do anything else that requires accessing the great library of knowledge in your brain, this is the state you want to be in. Patience is conducive to this state.

When someone experiences impatience, the body is tense and the mind is limited. This prevents clear thinking. This blocks your ability to remember and to utilize what you know.

Recall a moment when your mind was very alert. Where were you? What were you doing? What were you feeling? What were you telling yourself? What pictures where you visualizing? In the future when your mind is alert, consciously store this state in your mind and recall it to access it again.

Relax the muscles in your body. This is an important skill to master. As you breathe slowly and deeply, your muscles relax. As you visualize relaxing scenes, your muscles relax. You can choose scenes that you actually experienced in the past. And you can also choose imaginary scenes that you read about or have created on your own.

Studies have shown that slow music at sixty beats a minute, which is one beat each second, is conducive for accessing the state of alert mind, relaxed body. If someone finds it difficult to remember specific material, it is very worthwhile to play such music in the background since this enhances memory. Since your brain stores every state you are ever in, after creating this state with the appropriate slow music, you will find it easier to create this state on your own.

I used to be very nervous when I tried to remember information. I felt that I had a poor memory. And I proved it again and again. Because of my limiting belief about my memory, I immediately became tense when I tried to take in information that I needed to remember.

A tool that helped me immensely was one that was suggested to me by someone who had had the same problem and then overcame it. He told me that he would say to himself at the speed of one word a second, "Four, three, two, one. Alert mind, relaxed body." At first he would look at the seconds on a watch and say each word in a second. After a while, he did not need to look at his watch.

I found this tool amazingly helpful and I have shared it with many others who have also benefited. I now use this whenever I have to wait for someone or something.

PATIENCE IS AN EXPRESSION OF RESPECT

The Torah concept of the value of people is that each individual is created in the image of the Creator. An honorable person is the one who honors others (*Ethics of the Fathers* 4:1). Being impatient with another human being has aspects of disrespect. Being patient makes you a more honorable person yourself since your patience is an expression of your respect.

If someone was walking with a truly great person, and that great person was not moving as fast as one would have liked to go, it would be relatively easy to be patient. Walking with that person would be considered an honor and privilege. The fact that he is elderly and moving slower than you normally would just adds to your feelings of self-importance that you have an opportunity to be of service to this great human being. Every person you are patient with is an important person. Every human is created in the Almighty's image.

What if you have to repeat yourself many times? If the person you are repeating yourself to is someone of supergenius stature whose memory is not what it used to be because he had Alzheimer's, most people would feel it a privilege to be able to be of service to this genius whose brain is not functioning as it used to. Viewing each person you explain things to as a child of the Creator will make it much easier to be patient. The Almighty, your beloved Father and powerful King, is also the Father and King of the individuals you need to interact with. He is the One Who decides the intellectual capabilities of any specific person. If it is His will that the person you interact with should now have a brain that functions slower than yours does, your respect for that person is ultimately respect for the Creator.

Suppose you were scheduled to have a meeting with a brilliant and powerful leader. He is very busy and it was very difficult to schedule a meeting with you. But he agreed to meet you with the understanding that you might have to wait a long time until he was finished with the pressing issues and decisions that take priority. You were looking forward to this meeting for a long time. You consider it an honor to meet him even if you will have to wait five, six, even seven hours. While you are waiting for him, you keep thinking, "How fortunate I am to be able to have a meeting with someone I respect so much." When you have proper respect for each individual about whom the Talmud says, "A person is obligated to say, 'The world was created for me,'" you will find it easier to be patient.

The more self-respect you have for yourself, the easier it will be for you to be patient. Your value is immense since you are created in the image of the Creator, you are His child, and you are obligated to say, "The world was created for me." Having this profound self-respect will make it easier for you to master the beautiful attribute of patience. The benefits of this mastery are so great that someone as important as you definitely deserves it.

Many years ago I met a brilliant Torah scholar who was patient and respectful to each person he met. He was very busy and besides his scholarly pursuits, people came from far and near to seek his advice. He was asked, "What enables you to have so much patience for each person?"

"They are children of the Almighty. How can I not be respectful toward each one of them?" he replied as if it were the most obvious thing in the world.

17

THE TONE OF PATIENCE

The music of your voice when you speak impatiently is much different from the way you sound when you are coming from a place of inner peace or serenity. An angry tone of voice creates a different emotional reaction than a cheerful, upbeat tone of voice. Just as different musical sounds elicit different feelings, so too, your tone of voice will either make people feel better or worse.

Professional singers spend a great deal of time practicing the way they sing various songs. Every one of us who speaks to other people is a professional communicator. Even if we are not paid for speaking, communicating with other people is a major part of our lives. And our tone of voice will have an effect on the recipient of our communication. Practice speaking the way you would like to speak when challenges arise.

Gain greater awareness of the tones of voice of other people. Listen to the way people speak when they are joyous, when they are cheerful, when they are upbeat. Listen to the way people speak when they are calm and relaxed. And listen to the way people speak when they are impatient or angry. Let every positive tone of voice serve as a reminder for you to speak with a pleasant tone of voice to others. Let every negative tone of voice serve as a reminder for you not to speak that way to others.

I hadn't realized how awful my tone of voice sounded when I was irritated, impatient, or angry. But various members of my family were. One day I received a tape with a note: "Please listen to this tape to see how you frequently sound. We have asked you to speak more pleasantly many times. So far we have not been successful. Perhaps if you hear how you sound, you will be motivated to speak in ways we would appreciate."

That tape was bitter medicine, and it proved very effective. No way do I want to sound like that.

18

THE KINDNESS OF PATIENCE

People hate to be rushed. Some people are so nervous that others will rush them that they cannot think clearly when they need to ask a question or make a request. Tell this person, "Please take your time. Go at a pace that makes you comfortable." Observe the person and you will notice that there is an immediate reduction in tension. When you speak with someone on the telephone and hear from his tone of voice that he is anxious because he feels you are in a rush, you might say, "I have time right now." Then listen to his tone of voice becoming calmer.

Waiting for another person can be a major act of kindness. Miriam, Moses' sister, waited for him when he was an infant floating in a basket on the Nile. She wanted to make certain that he was safe. Many years later she was rewarded when the entire nation waited for her before traveling further in the Wilderness. Every time you wait patiently for someone, you are building up a merit that will benefit you measure for measure.

The more difficult an act of kindness, the greater the reward. You will be able to do some acts of kindness for someone without the need to be patient. Every act of kindness is precious. But the value of kindness that necessitates patience is especially great. If you are doing an act of kindness for someone and need more patience than you originally thought you would need, hear an inner voice saying, "The added value of the patience that I need now makes what I am doing more precious than it was originally." Internalizing this awareness will make it easier for you to be more patient.

When I was younger I felt a need to do as many kind acts for as many people as possible. It was like I was collecting something as a hobby, and I wanted to collect as many as possible.

It was pointed out to me a number of times, "You always seem in such a rush that you make some people feel very uncomfortable." I didn't take this feedback seriously. I felt that my approach was right and I couldn't help it if some people didn't like my style.

What changed me was that I found myself in a situation where I needed to ask favors from a number of people. I experienced that some people were patient with me while others where impatient. This brought home to me the importance of being patient when trying to help others. Patience itself is an integral part of the kindness.

19

ACTING "AS IF"

True patience emanates from within. When you are really patient, you experience it authentically. But what if you try your best and nevertheless are not yet able to really be patient? Does that mean you should act impatiently toward others until the great moment when you actually become patient?

There is a powerful principle that applies to many other traits and qualities as well as patience. Even before you actually become patient, you have a right to act as if you were patient. By acting as if you were patient, you are making an important step in the right direction. It is very likely that when you go through the motions of patience, it will become the real you. Even if this takes a long time, at least others will not suffer from your impatience.

"But if I act as if I were patient and I am really impatient, won't that just cause me more stress and tension?" A good question. And the answer is that, "Yes, it might. But it doesn't necessarily have to."

If someone acts as if he were patient and resents the need to do this, it is likely to add to the inner stress. But if you act as if you were patient as part of the process of mastering authentic patience, you can feel an inner sense of celebration that you are working on developing your character. These positive feelings that you choose to experience will increase the likelihood that you will integrate real patience.

When someone told me to act as if I were patient when I'm not, I became irritated. This didn't seem to me to be the honest thing to do.

"I must be true to my real feelings," I argued. "When I feel impatient, that's the way I want to act."

"Think it over by viewing the situation from the point of view of another person who needs to deal with you and is really impatient. Suppose you are concerned about a serious health issue and you consult a physician. If the doctor you visit is a very busy person, would you want his entire demeanor and tone of voice to reflect his impatience?"

"Of course not," I replied.

"Imagine asking a teacher to clarify a point and the teacher is really impatient. There is much material to cover and the teacher is running late. Would you want the teacher to act as impatiently as he feels when he explains the idea to you?"

I got it. I would appreciate someone making an effort to act as if he were patient even though this took an act of will and wasn't his spontaneous response. I'm certain others feel the same about me.

BREATHING SERENELY

Master the art of breathing serenely. Since you are continuously breathing the entire day, this is the most powerful and effective tool for creating the peaceful feelings that are conducive for patience.

In previous books we cited the Midrash on the last verse of *Psalms*. There we are told to praise the Almighty for each and every breath that we take. Those who practice this regularly already know the spiritual, emotional, and physical benefits. Breathing slowly and deeply with thoughts of gratitude releases stress and tension. Then one is able to create and access peaceful and joyous states.

As soon as you begin to feel impatient, let the feelings you experience be the start of your focusing on the gift of oxygen. As you exhale, feel all stress and tension leaving. As you inhale, feel the fresh oxygen traveling from head to toe relaxing every muscle and every cell in your entire body.

As you breathe, repeat the word, "Patience." Say it with gentle and soothing patience. As your brain is conditioned to associate slow breathing with patience, the very act of breathing slowly will continuously enable you to be more patient.

I used to be very impatient. I would tell myself to stop being so impatient, but this didn't change me.

One thing that made a major difference for me was the suggestion that I become more aware of how I breathe when I am impatient and to compare this with how I breathe when I am totally calm and relaxed. I realized that when I experience impatience I take many short breaths at faster than usual speed.

The next time I felt totally calm and relaxed, I realized that I was breathing slowly and deeply. Just changing the depth and speed of my breathing had a remarkable effect on my emotional state.

PATIENCE IS WITHIN YOU

There are always external factors that arise to challenge your state of patience. The source of patience is in your mind and brain. Therefore, regardless of the external situation or occurrence, you always have the ability to control the buttons and switches that create patience.

Pilots receive training on simulators. From the safety of the ground, they watch a screen. Based on what they see on the screen, they are required to make the right moves. After sufficient practice, they are able to make the right moves in actual life-or-death situations. The center of knowledge of what to do is already programmed in their brains. Even if new situations arise, the patterns of choices are imbedded in their brain cells.

You can view patience similarly. The external events are just tests. The way to pass these tests with patience is to go back to your brain and access your patience and wisdom.

Many people have benefited from the tool of touching their forehead when challenges arise. This reminds them that the inner resource of patience is at their fingertips. Experiment and see how this works for you.

I used to blame other people for causing me to become impatient. They go too slow. They make mistakes. They don't communicate appropriately. When I wouldn't be blaming other people, I would blame situations and circumstances. If everything out there would be the way I wanted it to be, I wouldn't become frustrated.

One day I was told, "Patience is in your mind." These five words were exactly what I needed to hear. Of course external factors are part of the picture. But that is an integral part of living on this planet. Blaming the external factors never made me more patient. Once I totally accepted the reality of creating patience in my own brain, I knew I was on the path to mastery of patience.

THIS MAKES ME IMPATIENT

What is the underlying message when someone says, "You cause me to become impatient," or, "This makes me impatient"? The assumption here is that another person or a specific situation is the cause of your impatience.

Impatience is a choice. It is one reaction out of many that can be chosen. If you put the blame on your becoming impatient on an external factor, you are to some degree giving up on your own power to create your reaction. Your reaction in any situation always depends on how you personally and subjectively evaluate and perceive that situation.

View your impatience as a choice. You will then find it easier to learn to react in new and better ways. You may make it your goal to master patience to such a degree that you will always choose patience over impatience. You may develop such a strong sense of humor that when others would become impatient, you actually enjoy the humor that can be found in the situation.

You can even choose to respond to situations that used to

elicit impatience with such reactions, "I will feel more and more empowered and creative every time this occurs." Isn't this arbitrary? It sure is and even though the reaction of impatience might be more automatic, empowerment and creativity are much better for you.

I met a person who told me that he has made it his lifelong commitment to help people upgrade their emotional responses and reactions to events, occurrences, and situations. He has found that by changing one's pattern of expressing the cause and effect of emotions, it will change one's attitude from passive victim of events to an active participant in how one chooses to react. He advises people to word their statements, "In the past I have chosen to react with irritation when this type of thing happened." Or, "In the past I used to choose impatience when I was kept waiting." This sends the underlying message, "I can presently make wiser choices."

23

THIS, TOO, WILL INCREASE MY PATIENCE

The way that you perceive a situation is the way that the situation will effect you. This is a fundamental principle that we have elaborated on in previous books. When thinking about increasing your level of patience, many potentially frustrating situations will be reframed as beneficial opportunities for character development.

Develop the habit of repeating, "This, too, will increase my patience." How often will you say this? The more impatient you are when you start this process, the more frequently you will find this beneficial. The problem itself will be the source of the solution.

Even if you are already quite patient by nature or through having developed this quality, challenging situations and challenging people may be sent your way to help you become even more patient than before. So you need not feel left out. If today you do not need more patience, you can gain patience by waiting patiently for other opportunities to increase your patience.

Do you have the patience right now to repeat to yourself, "This, too, will increase my patience," one hundred times? Do you have the patience to repeat this one hundred times each day for ten straight days? If you have the patience and you repeat this that many times, you will find yourself automatically repeating it when you need it. And if you do not yet have the patience to repeat it this amount of times, by repeating it you will find that, "This, too, will increase your patience."`

I found myself in a situation where I had to do many repetitive tasks that used to frustrate me greatly. I had great plans for what I eventually would like to do to earn money to support my family. What I was doing in the meanwhile was not even close to what I really wanted to do. The less I accomplished at work, the more exhausted I was when I came home.

It was suggested that I repeat often, "This, too, will increase my patience." This ensured me of accomplishing each and every day. I now was aware that I was building my character. The patience I acquired by doing things that I found boring enabled me to accomplish much more than I had imagined. And emotionally I consistently experienced the positive feelings that come with doing something meaningful.

24

STORE PATIENCE
IN YOUR BRAIN

The more patience in your brain, the easier it is to access this state. Consciously create more and more patient minutes. How do you do this? Read on.

When working on patience, daily spend three one-minute sessions being patient. You might want to do this during peaceful moments. Then the quality of your patience will be truly peaceful. Or you might prefer to do this during challenging moments. Then your stored patience will be moments when you were able to transcend potential impatience. Either way you will have stored patience in your brain.

Whenever you do this, designate an entire minute to being patient. Look at a watch and for sixty seconds repeat, "Right now I am being patient." Then do this later for another minute. And finally do this a third time.

Keep doing this three times a day for thirty days. At the end of a month, your brain will have experienced consciously putting itself in patient states ninety times. This creates a strong inner resource of patience that will be yours in challenging situations. Often the challenges that require patience are less than an hour in duration. Fortunately, you already have an hour and a half of patience stored away.

What if you need six hours of patience? Just run ninety minutes of patience the first hour and a half. Then start all over from the beginning and rerun those same ninety minutes once again. After you have done this, you just doubled your patience archives. Three hours of patience are now stored away. As you access those three hours, you will have the six hours that you needed now. After you do this, you will have six hours of patience stored in your brain for future use.

As you can see, this process will eventually give you an unlimited supply of patience.

25

IN ALL CONTEXTS

We have written previously (*Happiness: Formulas, stories, and insights*) that once you upgrade your brain in any context, you can now get a free upgrade in all contexts. This applies to happiness, to courage, to kindness, and likewise to patience. This powerful idea means that if you are able to create or access a state of patience in even one context, you can mentally transfer that state to all contexts.

In what contexts have you already been patient? Even the most impatient person will be able to think of a few. Realize that you now can access this very same patience in new contexts where you have not yet been as patient as you would have liked to be.

When you find yourself in a context where you become impatient, ask yourself, "In what context have I been patient?" Transfer that patience to the present. Once you have actually done so, you have vivid proof that you are able to be patient in new contexts. This gives you a powerful inner resource.

I used to think that I could only be patient in certain situations. There are many situations about which I would say, "I just don't have the patience for this."

What changed my attitude was when someone asked me to study with a student who was slower than me. I said, "I lack the patience for this." I thought that this was a good excuse.

But the person I said this to challenged me, "Do you mean to say that you have never been patient before about anything?"

"Of course I don't mean to say that," I replied. "I've been patient plenty of times."

"I thought so," he said. "Good. You didn't have surgery to remove those patient memories, did you?"

I smiled and got the point. I didn't feel like studying with this fellow and claiming that I lacked patience was a rationalization.

"Learn with this fellow, and you'll see that you will increase your level of patience," he said to me. "I'm only asking this of you because it is of utmost importance that this other student pass an upcoming exam."

I agreed and did so wholeheartedly. From then on whenever I saw that person he was a positive reminder to me that I can utilize all of my inner resources in all context. I have gained more from this awareness than the fellow I studied with.

26

IMAGINATION

Impatience is caused by imagination. And imagination will enable you to become more patient.

When we are experiencing impatience, it is often because we are picturing in our minds how we will be late, how we are losing out, how we would like to be somewhere else, and many similar mental pictures. Some people see these mental images clearly. Others just feel the feelings, while the actual pictures are not in their conscious mind. But the basis of these feelings is one's imagination.

Imagination is one of the most powerful tools you have. All great visionaries have a vision that drives them to turn their imagination into reality. Soon after the destruction of the Temple in Jerusalem, Rabbi Akiva was able to visualize the future rebuilding of the Temple. His emotional reaction was not based on the actual present reality, but on the future which was quite real in his imagination. The power of imagination prepared Rabbi Akiva to transcend being tortured to death by serenely reciting the *Shma Yisrael* prayer.

Your own imagination will enable you to visualize yourself having sufficient patience for all of the challenges that arise. Mentally run scenes of yourself being serenely patient. You do not need to see the pictures clearly and vividly. Just sit in one place imagining that you are watching yourself on a large screen being patient in many different contexts.

Let your imagination come up with scenarios that you may be faced with and in each and every scene see yourself with a calm look on your face experiencing inner peace. You may try looking at yourself in a mirror when you feel inner calm and relaxation. This is the look you will use as your model for creating images of patience.

I had read and heard a lot about the power of visualization. But I don't see mental pictures very clearly. So I would think, "This isn't for me." Then I was told by an expert at integrating skills and inner resources through visualization, "You don't need to see a picture clearly. Your brain is an amazing storehouse of thousands and thousands of pictures. Otherwise you wouldn't recognize anybody. You wouldn't even recognize your house. The only reason familiar objects and places are familiar is because you have mental pictures of them stored in your brain cells. You can practice visualizing yourself handling all kinds of difficult situations with your inner resources even if you don't actually see those mental movies. Just imagine that you are watching them." Utilizing this ability has transformed my life. I try to help as many people as I can by encouraging them to do the same.

"IF I WERE…"

If you experience impatience and do not find it easy to just change your state into patience, here is a tool that has proven helpful to many:

Ask yourself, "If I were actually patient right now, how would I think and what would I be feeling?" This question enables your brain to think the thoughts of patience and feel the feelings.

"If I were patient right now, how would I be breathing?" This helps you breath slower and deeper. As you do this, you immediately let go of tension.

"If I were patient right now, how would my muscles feel?" As you ask yourself this question, scan your muscles from head to toe. If you feel muscle tension anywhere, let those muscles become looser. You can easily tighten and loosen your hand muscles. With practice, you will be able to release muscle tension in your jaws, shoulder, arms, and anywhere else where you experience tension.

"If I were patient right now, how would I speak to this

person?" By asking yourself this question, you will be able to get in touch with how you speak when you are patient. Even if you are not yet able to totally speak in that manner right now, you will still communicate better than you would have otherwise.

Utilize this pattern for all other states that you want to access. For example, "If I were joyous right now, how would I feel and what would I be thinking?" "If I were courageous right now, how would I be feeling and how would I speak and act?" "If I were kind and compassionate right now, what would I say and do?"

28

IMAGINE YOURSELF BEING SUPER PATIENT

Imagine yourself as being a person who is the ultimate master of patience. You might imagine yourself being a specific person you have met or heard about. Or you can create a totally imaginary person who is joyous, courageous, creative, kind, and patient.

If you are being challenged with being patient on Friday afternoon, imagine that you are Hillel. It is not you who must be patient now. It is Hillel and he has already proven how patient he is. And you do not need to wait for a Friday afternoon experience; you can really imagine that you are Hillel any day of the week.

If you have to explain something to someone who needs many repetitions, imagine that you are Rabbi Praida, who repeated each idea four hundred times to a slow student. You personally might not yet have developed the patience to repeat the information so many times. But Rabbi Praida did. And when you are being Rabbi Praida you plug into his amazing ability to be patient.

Think of a person who challenges your patience the most. Who do you know who is able to be patient with this person? Imagine being that person. If you cannot think of any specific individual, imagine being a person who has developed patience to such an extent that it is always easy for that person to stay calm and clear thinking.

A similar approach is to imagine putting on the head of a person with the inner resource that you wish for yourself. For example, some people who prepare to take a difficult exam mentally put on the head of the teacher of the class. If you need to solve a complex problem, put on the head of someone who is an expert in this area. As regards patience, put on the head of a patient person. As you do this, the rest of your muscle system will follow along.

I don't have the patience necessary to study for tests. Whatever I remember from class is what I'll write on a test. I wanted to get better grades, but I felt that I wasn't patient enough. Then I heard about the idea of imagining that I was a patient person. I knew someone who enjoyed studying for tests and would remember the information for very long periods of time. I imagined that I was that person. This helped me study for the test in a way that I had never done before. When I took the test, I imagined that I was a student with total recall. The joy that I experienced from doing so well showed me that I could master this technique. I have used this in speaking in public and in writing essays. Before I tried this myself I wouldn't have believed that this would be so effective.

LIVE IN REALITY

"I shouldn't have to wait this long for a reply."
"This trip shouldn't be delayed for such a long a time."
*"The project should have been completed already. It didn't have
to take this long."*
"They should have been here already."
"The meeting should have started on time."

There are many situations when we wish that things would be different than they actually are. Because of this we feel frustrated and impatient. But the reality is that things are the way they are, aren't they? Now that this is so, we have to make a choice. Should I choose to feel the tension and distress of impatience? Or should I choose to feel some positive feeling? Viewing the situation from this perspective can make it easier for you to choose patience.

"But I don't want things to be the way they are!" we can keep repeating over and over again. But no matter how many times we repeat this it will not change the reality. We may be able to take some practical action to improve the situation. If that practical action is in the best interests of everyone involved, then this may be the wisest choice and that is the choice you should make. If, however, the actions you may take will cause you and others new problems, the wisest choice is to not take that action.

The wisest choice is never to sit or stand there and stew. The wisest choice is never to build up in your mind and emotions that the situation is so frustrating that you cannot take it any more, that you have reached your limits of patience and are now choosing to get angry and tense and stressed out and even furious. For a young child a tantrum might be what is appropriate for his age. If you are old enough to read this, then it is not appropriate for your age. But what if putting on a show of a tantrum is exactly what is needed to get people who should do something to actually do it? Then if that is your only option it might be the wisest choice. But don't bet on it. When you think creatively of options, you will almost always you will find a better choice. Thinking about the wisest option in the present is the wisest choice to make.

A parent shared this with me: My children frustrated me greatly. They were essentially very good. But they wouldn't help out in the house when and how they should have. Some liked to read and would continue reading even when we obviously needed their help. "I'll be there as soon as I finish this chapter," they would say. But as soon as one chapter was finished, they would begin the next one. Another child was totally unreliable about coming home on time. He wouldn't do anything seriously wrong, but a half hour was at least an hour and an hour could be two hours. I was totally patient with strangers, but not with my children. I would do a slow burn and scream at my children about how wrong they were acting.

I met a friend at a wedding and told him about my constant frustration and anger at home. "Live in reality," he told me. "I agree with you. It is the right thing for your children to listen to you and to do so right away. But they don't. So your actual issue right now isn't whether or not they should listen, but how you should react if they aren't listening and what you can do to motivate them in a way that creates and maintains a positive emotional atmosphere in the house."

That made sense to me. I needed to accept reality instead of fighting it. This enabled me to remain calmer even though I strongly wanted my children to react differently.

details

30

FOCUS ON YOUR GOAL

Whatever you focus on gets reinforced. Therefore, when you are working on patience, keep your main focus on increasing patience. Those who keep focusing on instances of impatience, strengthen the quality that they do not want.

This is similar to saying to yourself, "I don't want to think of the color green," and then repeating this over and over again. "Just not green. Green is what I don't want. Any other color besides green." It's obvious from reading this that if all you think about is not thinking of green, that is exactly what you are thinking about. If you don't want to think about green, focus on yellow, red, orange, or blue.

What is true for colors is true for patience. Keep talking about patience. Keep focusing on times and moments when you have been patient in the past, are patient in the present and plan to be even more patient in the future.

At the end of the day, remember that day's moments of patience. This will make it easier for you to see yourself as a person who has already been patient many times. Each day you will be able to add additional examples of having been patient and this creates a positive loop that keeps getting stronger.

I grew up being told I was very impatient. I noticed many instances when this was true. I would often say to myself, "There I go again being impatient." I didn't want to be impatient. And I was puzzled as to why my repeating to myself, "I don't want to be impatient," wasn't helping me become more patient.

I asked an expert on character development for his explanation why I wasn't improving even though it was so important to me.

"Whatever you consistently focus on gets stronger," he explained. "Your brain stores these memories and the neural pathways that are used most often become thicker. This makes it easier to rerun the same route. If someone would want to increase impatience, the way to do it is to keep talking about all the times he has already been impatient and how he is afraid that he might be impatient in the future. To master patience, which I see as your real goal, keep focusing on thoughts and memories of patience."

Realizing what I needed to do enabled me to work on this effectively.

31

COLLECT RESOURCEFUL STATES

There is a hobby that has the ability to transform lives. Collect resourceful states. By making a personalized list of positive, life-enhancing states you can reread your list whenever you need to wait. This way you will experience your favorite states over and over again. Instead of being in the unresourceful state of impatience, you will be calmer, more upbeat, in good spirits, more empowered, more alive and energized.

When you remember times and moments when you were in specific states, remember what you were saying to yourself, the mental pictures you saw, the feelings you felt. Remember your way of breathing, speaking, and your body language. This enables you to experience those same states. The more intense the original experience and the more vivid the memory, the stronger that state will now be. Be patient. This adds up. The more times you are joyous, the easier it is to access joy. The same with confidence, courage, serenity, and every single positive state.

Label your positive, resourceful states as you experience them. This will make it easier for you to retrieve those states from the mental library of your brain. Giving your states personalized names will make it easier for you to have greater state management.

Besides listing standard names such as a state of joy, serenity, courage, determination, concentration, and being energized, create labels that are uniquely yours. For example, if you felt total calm while watching the gentle ocean waves, you now have a "Watching the ocean waves state." If you had a great victory, you can label it, "Winning the grand prize." Remember times you smiled and laughed and you have a "Smiling and laughing state." If a spoon or other item falls down, you can have a "Gravity is still working state." If you just missed a bus by a few seconds, you can access your, "I can see!" state.

Have a separate list for the unresourceful states you experience. Instead of saying, "I'm in an awful mood today," you can say, "Right now, I'm in a nervous state." Or, "Ah, this is my impatient state." Or, "Yeah, I'm in an irritated state." Do not resist. Just experience it and you will find it easier to gently access more resourceful states.

Remember your most precious memories of the past. Turn them into states to access at will. I personally have a state of my teacher, Rabbi Mordechai Gifter, saying to me over forty years ago on the day I entered his office for my entrance exam, "Good morning, Zelig. How are you today?"

Your most spiritually elevated moments are states. Label them. Your favorite songs are states. Inspiring speakers are states. Words of wisdom are states. Great people you can model are states. For example, your Hillel state will enable you to access a specific type of patience. And your "Rabbi Praida state" will enable you to repeat ideas over and over again until they are understood.

When will you find the time to read your state list? Whenever you are faced with a challenging situation, you can read it. Whenever you want to mentally prepare yourself to be at your best, you can read it. And whenever you feel the irritation of your impatient state, you can read your list of your greatest and favorite states. After a while, the resourceful states will be an automatic and spontaneous aspect of your personality.

Those who will gain the most from collecting states are the individuals who will calmly be more aware moment by moment of their specific states. The unresourceful states will be stepping stones for accessing life-enhancing resourceful states.

32

MODEL AND MORPH

Learn from the patience of others. Every person you see who is patient in situations that challenge you serves as a role model for how you too can be patient.

As you observe the body language, manner of speaking, and word content of patient people, you have a picture of what you need to do to become more patient yourself.

As you experiment with the patterns of the patient people you observe, you will be able to ask yourself, "What beliefs and attitudes do I need to internalize to make this my reality?"

When possible, interview patient people and ask them to share the beliefs and thought patterns that over time have enabled them to maintain patience.

Morph! What is morphing? It is when you see a picture of yourself taking over the new patterns of behavior of someone else. How do you model and morph? Mentally run the picture of someone you have seen who is a model of patience. See that person on a screen in your mind as if you were watching a film on a real screen. Rerun the scene over and over again.

You do not need to see the scene clearly to do this. You can even do this unconsciously by acting as if you were staring at a screen. Then morph. That is, see yourself in the picture the way you have previously seen your role model. In a relatively short time you can rerun these scenes hundreds of times in your magnificent brain.

After you see that you can do this with patience, repeat the process with joy, enthusiasm, kindness, courage, and every other positive state, pattern, and skill you want to acquire.

I used to look at many of the positive behaviors of others and say to myself, "I wish I could do that. But that's just not me." And the quality I felt I needed the most was patience. But what could I do? I had been impatient since I was a child, and I didn't think I could change very easily.

What changed this was a meeting I had with someone who was a master at learning from the positive patterns of others. He told me that the number one skill he cherished the most was the ability to observe someone's patterns and then to mentally visualize himself behaving similarly.

He told me to model and morph him. I did. This gave me the powerful awareness that just as this person was able to model and morph others, I could model and morph him to integrate his awareness that I could do the same for every attribute and behavior I wanted for myself. Not only did this help me become more patient, this also enabled me to develop skills and talents that I previously wouldn't have imagined being mine.

33

PRAY FOR PATIENCE

You do not have to do it alone. Your loving Father and powerful King, Creator and Sustainer of the universe, is waiting to help you. Pray to Him. Ask Him for help in mastering patience. Ask Him for the strength to be patient with His other children. Ask Him for the strength to be as patient as necessary to serve Him with joy and love. Ask Him for the strength for the patience to gain all the knowledge and skills to make the most of your stay on this planet.

I recently attended the wedding of the youngest child of a rabbi in Jerusalem. With great joy at this celebration he publicly expressed his profound gratitude to the Almighty that he reached this moment. He related the story of a great man who married off his youngest child. This was the sixteenth wedding in that family. He called all of the members of his family together and said, "I have now raised and married off sixteen children. And this happened without the help of the Almighty." Of course, when he said this everyone was puzzled and confused how he could say this. Then he continued, "The

Almighty did everything. I couldn't have done any of this myself. It wasn't just help from the Almighty. It was totally Him and Him alone."

This concept is what we need to master patience. The Almighty waits for us to be the way He would want us to be. Let us ask Him for the Divine attribute of patience. Let your personal prayer for patience be frequently on your lips.

I was ruining my life and the life of my family with my constant impatience. I tried and tried to become more patient, but I was a total failure. It seemed to me that the more I tried, the less successful I was. I came to the realization that I couldn't become more patient through my own efforts. I started to pray specifically for the patience I so desperately needed. Every time I was faced with a challenge, and to me everything was a challenge, I said a personal prayer:

"Please, G-d, bless me with patience. You have the power and ability to give me the patience I need right now."

Before I went to sleep at night, I asked for patience for the next day. When I woke up in the morning, I prayed for patience for that day.

I saw how my sincere prayers were answered. I experienced patience in a way that was impossible for me before. I would express my gratitude to G-d after each success. This entire process gave me a greater understanding of the power of prayer.

THE PATIENCE CLUB

Become a member of The Patience Club. To join, all you need to do is to decide, "I am now a member of The Patience Club. And the next session of this club starts this moment."

You do not have to pay any dues to join The Patience Club. You do not have to travel. You do not have to influence and persuade anyone else to attend sessions. You are automatically and immediately in a session whenever you decide it is the right time.

Knowing that at the same time you are involved in a session there are other members who are also being patient will give you added strength and encouragement. At any given moment there are many people on our planet who are patient. Every time someone is patient, they become an automatic member of the club for as long as they maintain their patience. Even those who are not aware of the club have honorary membership during the time they are patient. So when you consciously join the club, you are a part of a worldwide club.

The people who could gain the most from joining this club are those who are still highly impatient. If you know an impa-

.ient person with a sense of humor, you might suggest that he become a member of the club. If he lacks a sense of humor, he might not find it amusing to be told of the club. If so, he really needs it. But you need the patience to find a creative way to motivate him to join.

If an entire family likes the idea of The Patience Club, and they are experiencing impatience, any member of the household can announce, "The Patience Club is now in session." If it appears that that it will take a few minutes for people to calm down, one can even say, "The Patience Club's session will begin in five minutes." Then everyone can remain impatient for five more minutes.

35

RAISING CHILDREN WITH PATIENCE

I grew up in an impatient home. Well, it was not exactly the home that was impatient, but my parents. Both my father and mother lost their patience quickly, way too quickly. They were good parents, they cared for our welfare, but their impatience led to much anger. The emotional atmosphere in our home was frequently stormy, and tension was the norm. They would tell us that we behaved worse than any other children they knew. Later on I realized that this wasn't true, but impatience leads to anger and anger caused them to say things that one should never say to a child.

"Be patient with your children." This theme repeats itself when you ask parents who have raised large families about the advice they would give new parents.

What is the difference between growing up in a home with patience and a home where this is consistently lacking? It is the difference between walking in a beautiful garden when the weather is perfect or walking in a torrent of rain on a muddy road at night. It is the difference between listening to harmonious music or hearing trash-can lids banging together. It can be the difference between having a safe haven where you are respected and loved or feeling like you are among enemies who torment you. Is the distinction really this sharp? Yes.

A parent who is impatient teaches impatience to the children. When children are impatient, they kvetch more. When they want something from their parents, they demand service and they want it right away. Their impatience will make their impatient parents even more impatient. And then the way the parents speak and act towards their children implant impatience even more deeply.

Regardless of how impatient any parent has ever been in the past, right this moment they can make a decision to be more patient. Right now a parent can say, "I am totally resolved to be patient. I will do whatever it takes to master patience with my children."

Impatient parents who transform themselves into patient parents are teaching their children an important lesson: "We can change." We can develop positive character traits even if it means developing a quality we had not had before. This will be a lesson that goes beyond just patience. It can be applied to every character trait that exists. This is such an important legacy to give to one's children that this alone can motivate a parent to make every effort possible to master patience.

Parents spend much time, energy, and money on their children. The extra investment of becoming patient themselves is minor when we contemplate the extent of the benefits in health, emotions, and spirituality.

Isn't it wonderful to contemplate how you would react now if you knew that one day your children would look back and say, "What I appreciate most about my parents is that they were consistently patient with me"? And if they cannot say that yet, your presently working on patience will enable them to say, "What I respect and appreciate about my parents is they worked on themselves to master patience."

36

FOLLOW THROUGH TO REACH YOUR GOALS

"I've set so many goals for myself that I didn't reach that I am reluctant to make new goals. Why cause myself more disappointment?"

"I would be a major scholar now if I would have followed through on my learning goals. Unfortunately, I am far from where I have the potential to be."

"I have a number of projects that I am working on. But I get bored and prefer to start new ones rather than complete what I have already started."

The only way to accomplish in life is to set goals for yourself and to consistently strive to reach them. Without clear goals, a person does not focus his energy on the specific actions that need to be taken. Many people make goals in the important areas of their lives, but fail to reach them. What is missing? They need the patience to follow through.

Those who are willing to do whatever it takes to reach their goals put in the necessary time, work, and energy. The quality that will enable you to do so is patience. How much patience do you need? Just enough to complete what you began.

Every goal you reach enables you to believe in your ability to follow through until you successfully complete what you begin. Looking back you will be able to tell yourself, "I see that I had the patience to keep on going."

What one goal can you make for yourself right now that will make an important difference in your life? Imagine that you were given as much patience as you needed to reach this goal. Mentally run through the picture of your having persisted until you reached your goal. Feel the great joy of accomplishing in a meaningful way. And when you reach your goal know that the patience you have stored up in your brain is a resource you can patiently access whenever you need it.

I met an elderly person who has accomplished much more in life than most people ever thought he would. I have made it a habit to ask successful people, "What enabled you to accomplish as much as you did?"

"I can answer your question with one word," he said to me. "Patience."

"And that's it?" I asked him.

"By asking this question I see that you don't realize the power of patience," he said with a smile. "Without patience, you won't get

anywhere. If you have patience, you have everything."

"What about intelligence?" I asked him.

"The vast majority of people have a greater amount of intelligence than they utilize," he replied. "When you are patient, you access the knowledge you need. When you are patient, you persevere until you reach your goals. Be patient and you will be able to accomplish every goal that is humanly possible for you."

I saw that this worked for him and it makes sense that it will work for others.

PRACTICING UNTIL MASTERING

The mastery of important skills takes practice. Why doesn't everyone practice enough to attain mastery? Because it takes patience to keep on practicing. Often when people say, "I can't do that very well," what they are saying is, "I haven't yet expended the necessary time and energy practicing this skill until I can do it well."

"Everyone can learn every skill if they take it step by step and keep practicing." Those who believe this will be able to master more skills than those who believe, "There are things I can do and things that I can't. And what I can't do, I just can't do, and there's nothing I can do to change that."

There are definitely things that are impossible for each of us. Every mortal has limitations. But skills can be learned and mastered. Yes, some people are physically stronger than others. Some people are more musical, some more artistic, some have better memories and some are more creative. But in each of these areas the right method of practice will enable those with a lack of natural talent and skill to gain greater skill than they originally thought possible. We all have been surprised to find that we were able to effectively do things we thought we could not do.

Is it worth the time and effort for every individual to try to gain every single skill that others have? Of course not. We all have a limited amount of time on this planet and we need to make the most of it. But if a skill is valuable and important to you, realize that with sufficient patience to practice you will be able to acquire it. You may need to find a mentor who is appropriate for you. There are many teaching styles. Be patient until you find the teacher who meets your requirements. Then keep on practicing.

I needed to gain a few skills that I lacked in order to keep a job. I practiced but I felt totally tired, even exhausted, as soon as I began to practice. I spoke to a knowledgeable friend.

"I have a problem," I told him. "I know that I need to practice many times. But I hate to practice."

"Let's transform your problem into a goal," he said to me. "Your goal is to enjoy practicing. What have you been telling yourself as you practice?"

At first I wasn't aware of my thoughts. But then I realized that I was telling myself, "Why do I have to practice so much? Others seem to catch on faster."

"It doesn't make a difference whether others need less practice than

you or more. Your emotional reality will depend entirely on what thoughts go through your mind. Mentally create an enjoyable attitude while you practice. Sing to yourself. Play enjoyable music. Visualize great scenes. Imagine yourself being someone who loves to practice. Learn from the most successful people in sports. They all practice countless hours. Master the ability to enjoy practicing, and you will experience greater joy in your life. Practice creating joy at the same time you practice any other skill."

This worked for me and what used to cause me distress is now a major source of joy in my life.

TIME IS RELATIVE

When you enjoy yourself, time seems to go faster than it actually does. When you experience distress, time seems to go slower than usual. The more pleasure you have while you are waiting, studying, or are involved in some activity, the easier it will be for you to be patient.

If you have to do something that you do not enjoy, find ways to make it more enjoyable. Think of ways that you are helping others and feel the pleasure of doing acts of kindness. Use your creativity and imagination. Think of a context when you would enjoy this task.

At times you may not find a task or job intrinsically interesting, but you can listen to music or an inspiring tape. View your situation as, "I am enjoying the music or the ideas I am hearing. At the same time, my hands are occupied taking care of a task I need to get done." Visualize the music or the ideas as what you are "really" doing. The task is just a background form of doodling.

Think of a time when you were totally absorbed in what

you were doing. It may have been a long conversation you once had when you were totally absorbed or an extremely fascinating book you were reading or being involved in a creative process. When you looked to see what time it was, you were surprised at how time flew by. Utilize your memories of these instances to create even more instances of being totally absorbed. By increasing your level of skill at being able to do this at will, you will gain greater mastery at being able to transform feelings of impatience into patience.

If you are feeling impatient in a situation and you will have to be in this situation for a while, ask yourself, "What can I do now or focus on that will be more pleasurable?" As you come up with solutions, instead of distressful time moving slowly, you will find pleasurable time moving along swiftly.

When I'm bored with what I'm doing, I don't have the patience to keep at it. I keep looking at my watch and get a feeling that something is wrong with it. More time than has registered must have gone by. But when I check it with a highly reliable clock, I see that my watch is accurate.

I met a person who told me that he is almost never bored. "How do you do it?" I asked him.

"First of all, I am always happy that I am alive," he said to me. "And as long as I am alive, I have access to the creativity of my brain. I keep learning new things and I find this very exciting. I mentally create enjoyable scenes wherever I am. I mentally visualize myself master-

ing the positive patterns I wish to have. I see myself full of enthusiasm and excitement. I still am bored once in a while, and I use this to gain greater appreciation for all the other times when I'm not bored."

I didn't enjoy cooking. I used to become very impatient that the process of preparing food for my family took so long. Then I heard the concept that every act of kindness for one's family is a positive, spiritual action that one can do with joy. This elevated the way I looked at what I was doing and I had more patience than I ever did before. I also tried out new recipes and began to enjoy gaining greater expertise, becoming an excellent cook.

I used to be very bored with my mundane job. I was totally impatient waiting for the hour when I could go home. I didn't view myself as imaginative. But someone suggested to me that I could playfully imagine various scenarios that would add excitement to my life. For example, one day I imagined that I lived five hundred years in the past. For one day I would be given the opportunity to live in the future. Another day I imagined that I was lost in the middle of a desert. Suddenly I found myself sitting at this desk with plenty of water. I didn't tell others about these far out imaginative scenes. But I enjoyed myself beyond what I imagined I would and have become unbelievably patient.

BROADEN YOUR PATIENCE BASE

It is common for people to be more patient than usual with some individuals and less patient than usual with others. By becoming aware of the distinctions, you will be able to increase your patience with more people.

What is it about the people with whom you are more patient that allows you to be so with them? Some people are patient with young children. Since it is the very nature of the young to be limited, this is what one expects. Therefore it is easier to be patient. Others are more patient with their professional clients and customers. Since this is how they earn their living, the financial gain enables them to be patient since it serves their own interests. Yet others are patient with the elderly. They respect people who are older than they are. Also, they hope to live to an old age. They feel that their patience with these people is an investment in deserving to be treated with patience when they reach the same stage in life.

Learn from your patience with the individuals with whom you are most patient. Apply the same mind set and inner feelings with the people you are not yet patient with.

Now think about those with whom you are the least patient. What can you learn from the people you are patient with to be more patient with those you have lacked patience for until now?

If you are more patient with people who are handicapped, realize that every person is handicapped in some way. With some people it is more recognizable and with others less so. Even someone who is brilliant might be distracted and cannot concentrate right now as sharply as usual. Another person may be ill and you are not aware of this. But that is the reason they take longer to do what you feel they should be doing more quickly.

Always keep in mind that there may be factors which would allow you to be more patient. If you can think of specific common factors, it will make it easier for you. Even if you are not clearly aware of factors, you might say to yourself, "Since it is possible that I could view this person in a way that would make it possible for me to be patient, I'll decide to be at my optimal level of patience."

Based on a technique of Rabbi Simcha Zissel Ziv of Kelm, I practiced the following. I had a clear picture in my mind of someone I am always patient with. If I ever feel impatient with someone, I visualize the face of the person with whom I am easily patient. They are both created in the Creator's image so they automatically have a lot in common.

WHEN HAVE YOU BEEN EXTREMELY PATIENT?

L earn from your greatest moments of strength. This applies to all positive resources and patterns. When have you been the most patient for the longest periods of time? Regardless of the external factors that enabled you to be this way, it is a lesson to you of your potential to be patient.

Some people enjoy fishing. An integral aspect of fishing is to patiently wait for a fish to be hooked. Being impatient will not influence the fish to hurry up and be caught. Everyone who is patient when it comes to fishing also can apply this to people.

Some people enjoy playing chess. In chess one person makes a move, then he has to wait patiently until the other person decides to make his move. Each player keeps weighing his options. In chess one needs to develop the patience to weigh as many options as possible and the patience to wait for the other person to make his move. Is every chess player patient in all contexts? I never made a study of this. But each has the potential to be equally patient with people in other contexts. If one fails to do so, it is by choice, the choice of not yet developing this skill in more areas of one's life. Since it is a choice, one can make the decision: "I can be patient when playing chess. So I can likewise be patient with other people the rest of the time."

The parent of an infant looks forward to that child's wedding. It will take many years until the child is old enough to get married. No matter how high a priority this would be, the parent has to wait. Most other things one needs to be patient about will not take as long to accomplish. So if you are able to be patient for this, you can be patient for many other things.

When I used to think about being patient, I would immediately recall times when I was impatient. Since those instances were distressful, they came to the forefront of my mind whenever I heard the word "patience."

I was advised, "It's much wiser to think of your successes and learn from them. When are you patient?"

I buy a lottery ticket once a week. Every once in a while, I think about the joy I will experience if I win. Since the actual chances of winning are remote, I delay checking if my numbers won or not. Until I check them, I can still enjoy thinking that I might have won. I realize that this form of pleasure is not for everyone. But it does build up my ability to be patient.

ENJOY THE PROCESS

Enjoy the process of working on your patience quotient. It would be counterproductive for someone to say to himself, "Only when I am totally patient all the time will I be able to feel that I accomplished something." Rather, enjoy the entire process of working on mastery of patience. Even at the beginning stages, enjoy working on the project.

Whenever you are working on any project or goal, enjoy the process. The way to become impatient is to think, "I have a great deal to do to finish my project or reach my goal. I must feel anxious until I finally arrive at my destination." The way to patience is to think, "Life is made up of a series of projects and goals. I will enjoy the involvement. Each step I take in the right direction will give me pleasure."

When reading a book, some people have one goal: "I must finish this." Then everything up to that goal is just an annoyance that must be tolerated. Learn to enjoy each page and each sentence. When you enjoy what you read, you enhance your power to recall what you have read. Calm and relaxed feelings help you concentrate and understand what you have read.

Every child who enters the first grade has many years ahead until he graduates from the twelfth grade. This takes time. Imagine what it would be like to go through six years of elementary school thinking, "I want to graduate high school already. This is taking a long time. I want my waiting to be over." Compare that with the child who thinks, "I will enjoy graduating. And I will enjoy the process of learning and growing up. Every day of my life is an adventure. Every day of my life is a gift. I will enjoy and benefit every moment along the way."

We are all children of the Almighty. We have to make a choice in life. Will we or won't we enjoy the process of growing and learning?

Imagine that you have a choice of buttons to press. One button has a sign, "Be impatient the entire time you are working on a goal until you complete it." The other button has a sign, "Be patient and enjoy the entire time you are working on a goal until you complete it." It is obvious which button we would all choose.

Your brain is under your control. Enjoy the process of learning to control it the way you would control the buttons of a computer. Enjoying this process will enable you to enjoy all the other processes you are engaged in. And life is one big process.

I asked the head of a large organization to allow me to interview his employees. I wanted to discern which are the essential factors of those who are consistently frustrated and those who are basically calm and relaxed.

The key factor I found could be summarized by saying, "Those who just wanted to finish the project or the day were more irritable and tense. Those who enjoyed the entire process of the work they did were in enjoyable states the majority of the time."

I tried to teach those who didn't enjoy the process to begin to do so. Those who succeeded in integrating this pattern reported that they feel that they are living in an entirely different world than before.

EXPECT THINGS TO TAKE LONGER THAN YOU EXPECT

f we expect something to take fifteen minutes and it takes ten minutes, we react positively. If, however, we expect something to take five minutes and it takes ten minutes, we are likely to feel impatient. Our expectations are a key factor whether or not we will be patient.

The above leads to the following formula: Always expect things to take longer than you expect and you will find it easier to remain patient.

I am writing this while waiting in line in a bank. I need to cash a check. The bank teller did not have the necessary amount. We are waiting for the arrival of the manager who has the key to the bank's vault. I personally do a lot of my writing and editing while waiting. Since I usually expect to wait and am prepared to make use of this time, unless I am in a specific rush, I take these things in stride. Those who have unrealistic expectations about waiting become impatient quickly. After the manager arrived, the bank teller apologized for the wait. The apology was not necessary. I had the ideal illustration of the formula I had just written.

How long should things actually take? This, of course, is an unanswerable question. What things? What is the entire context? How long does this specific thing usually take? The actual answer is that things take as long as they do. Inefficiency slows things down and efficiency speeds things up. Frequently factors arise that will cause us to wait longer than usual. We still need to make assumptions about how long things might take. But remember to keep in mind: The actual time this will take will only be known after the fact.

Your initial assumption about how long anything will take is only a possibility. Living in reality means that if you were to have known how long something will actually take, that is the amount of time you should have expected it to take. So it can be stated that expecting things to take less time than they do is a failure to live in reality. We are not prophets and we cannot know exactly how long things will take. But we can say with total assurance: This will take as long as it takes. Fight the losing battle of demanding that it take less time and you will experience impatience. Live in reality and the serenity of patience will be yours.

I was always late for appointments, meetings, and the beginning of lectures. Again and again I would assume I could accomplish more in less time than it actually took.

"It's not my fault I'm late," I would constantly excuse myself. "Things took longer that they should have."

This caused me a lot of distress. Whenever I would have to wait for other people, it would make me late for the next thing I had on my schedule. I was impatient with others since I knew that if they didn't move at top speed I would be late for the next things I had to take care of.

One person I often kept waiting finally said to me, "Since things always take longer than you expect, it makes sense to expect them to take longer. Add this to the amount of time you assume that things will take."

What he said to me seems quite obvious. But being used to the pattern I had always followed, I didn't realize this until it was pointed out to me. Having had this pattern myself, I easily notice it in others. I try to help them by sharing what it took me so long to learn myself.

STAY CENTERED IN THE FACE OF IMPATIENCE

One of the most valuable states to master is the state of being centered. In this state, you feel that the focus of your energy is right in the balanced center of your being. When you are in a centered state, your mind is clear and you are able to handle well the various challenges that arise.

Impatience can be contagious. An encounter with an impatient person can easily throw someone off balance. That person's negative energy can effect the energy of the person on the receiving end of that impatience. The antidote is to stay centered. Then you can access a centered, focused, and flowing state. When your sense of being centered is strong, the uncentered energy of that person will be deflected. Even more, your being centered can have a positive effect on that person's emotional state.

When speaking to someone who is uncentered, keep your intended outcome in mind. What do you want your words to accomplish? You want to say things that express your thoughts and feelings and at the same time to have a calming effect on this person. Focus on the outcome you want. Only say words conducive to attain and maintain that outcome. Without thinking about your intended outcome, you are likely to say things that make the situation worse. I frequently tell people, "It's not that if you focus on outcome thinking, you will always say the right thing. It's that if you don't focus on the outcome and you are upset, you are going to say things that are counterproductive."

Make a motion with your hands that for you represent a centered state. Access or create a centered state and repeat your hand signal for this state. You might find it beneficial to observe someone you consider to be centered and to model that person's state. The more often you enter your centered state, the easier it will be for you to access it with your hand motions even when strong challenges arise.

My spouse and I are both high-powered people. We want to accomplish a lot in our lives and have strong personalities. When either one of us is impatient, the other easily becomes this way also. A teacher of ours kept telling us to focus on the outcomes we wanted and only say those things that would get us there. This sounded great when we were calm. But when we weren't, all those lessons went down the drain.

Finally, our teacher told us, "You need to keep repeating the words, 'Centered. Outcome thinking,' at least a thousand times a day. That means, that at least ten times a day repeat this as a song one hundred times each session. The actual time you spend on this is brief when you consider its benefits."

The way he said this to us showed us that he meant business. He threatened to reprimand us like we were never reprimanded before if we didn't follow through on this suggestion.

The difference that this made in our lives was fantastic. Will we keep it up? If we want our lives to be joyous and spiritual, we will. The consequences of the opposite is a form of mental torture.

SOME THINGS CANNOT WAIT

Patience is not always appropriate. There are some things that cannot wait. Medical emergencies need to be taken care of immediately. What ordinarily might be considered rude or insensitive would be totally appropriate to save someone's life. If you need to raise your voice and pound on a desk to convey that a situation is an emergency, that is what you must do. Snatching a public phone from someone who is not ready to let you use it to call an ambulance when a person's life is in danger is not polite, but it is your obligation to do so.

If you need to make a payment immediately or you will lose your home, you cannot wait. But how often have you actually found yourself in similar situations?

Yesterday I was in a rush, but not a major one. I took a taxi instead of a bus, and did not say anything to the driver about reaching our destination quickly. It was much more important for me that the driver would drive carefully than with speed. While he did not go faster than the speed limit, he tried to bypass some cars in a way that was not legal and a policeman gave him a ticket. Not only did it cost him money, but he wasted a lot of time. Trying to save seconds cost him about fifteen minutes. If he were to have known the outcome of his impatience, he would have realized that he could easily have waited.

"I can't wait." This used to be one of my favorite sentences.

"What will happen if you do?" someone who recently became a co-worker challenged me. This exchange happened a number of times the first month we were working together.

I realized that most of the time I really could wait, just that I don't feel like it.

Now, one of my favorite sentences is: "What will actually happen if I do wait?" It has given me a clearer picture of reality.

FROM THE OTHER PERSON'S POINT OF VIEW

Patient people are often experts at perceiving situations from the point of view of other people. Entering the mental world of those you interact with makes it easier for you to be more tolerant of their patterns of speech and behavior.

Some people may ask you the same questions over and over again. You may become impatient with them. They have the intelligence to understand what you said. Why do they keep repeating these questions? When you enter their mental world, you may realize that they are insecure and need reassurance or that something is weighing on their minds and they are distracted. Understanding them will enable you to be more patient.

People who care deeply about you may worry about your health and welfare. They may keep reminding you to eat properly, get enough rest, not do things that would be harmful or dangerous. You may initially react with impatience, "Not again. I've heard this many times already." But when you enter the mindset of the other person, you realize that this is a caring message.

You may feel impatient with an elderly person who speaks or acts too slowly for your comfort. But if you were to enter his world, you would understand his personal frustration and distress at not being agile, competent, and effective as he used to be. This compassion for him will make you more patient.

When you interact with someone who sincerely tries to understand your mental world, let it serve as a reminder to enter the world of others. And if you have a distressful interaction with someone who does not perceive you accurately and does not even try, let it serve as a reminder to you for the importance of your trying to understand people by entering their mindset.

I interviewed a teacher who won an award for his excellence in teaching.

"What are the key factors that made you such a great teacher?" I asked him.

"I was a slow student. Most teachers weren't as patient with me as I needed. Now that I am a teacher, whenever I see that a student has difficulties understanding, I enter his mind and emotions. This automatically makes it easier for me to be patient with him."

THINK BEFORE YOU SPEAK

Speaking without thinking is easy. It takes patience to think before you speak. This form of patience is wisdom since: "Who is wise? The one who foresees the outcome."

When you speak to someone who is easy to anger, you need to ask yourself, "What shall I say to bring out the best in this person?" Certain ways of speaking are likely to elicit this person's anger. Speaking with respect and addressing this person's needs will enable the person to remain calm. Have the patience to think of your wisest options.

No one likes to be insulted, and some people are more easily hurt than others. The more sensitive someone is, the more careful we need to be. Have the patience to select a pattern of speech that is an expression of respect.

Timing is often important. Yes, you should speak up, but not right now. You may need to wait until someone unwinds, lets off steam, rests, or is in a generally more open frame of mind. Ask yourself, "Is now a good time to say what I want to say?" If not, patiently wait until the time is right.

Every time you think before you speak, you are increasing your level of patience. Therefore you not only benefit in your present communication, but in everything you do in the future. The seconds you spend right now are a worthwhile investment.

"There are so many people who are difficult to get along with," I complained.

"I used to feel that way," my new acquaintance told me. "One new habit transformed that for me. I practiced thinking before I speak. First of all, this has helped me speak in a calm tone of voice. Also, by wording my sentences in ways that express sincere respect, I have been able to bring out the best in people."

I was determined to master this habit. At first I found it extremely difficult. But as I saw the benefits, it became surprisingly easier.

YOU WON'T LOSE OUT

Some people are afraid that if they become patient, they will not accomplish as much and their requests will not be fulfilled. But this is not accurate. To accomplish, you need to set goals and follow through. As we have written, the more patience you have, the more persistent and persevering you will be.

And what about the fear that people will not do what you request if you are patient? This is a fallacy. If someone likes you, he will be more receptive to meeting and even anticipating your requests. The more you sincerely like other people and care about them, to that degree they will more readily reciprocate.

When you are in a position of authority, you do not need to be impatient for people to follow your instructions and requests. At times your tone of voice may need to be slightly firmer than usual. For those who think that they need to express impatience or anger before others will listen to them, the question is, "Why do you feel that you can only influence,

– 120 –

lead, and persuade by causing distress?" There are many positive and pleasant approaches that are effective. If you do not yet apply them, read up on the subject. Observe master communicators who are consistently pleasant. Seek out a coach.

If you do feel that you will lose out by being patient, it is worthwhile writing down a specific list of what you feel you will lose. Then think of alternative ways to accomplish and achieve patiently what you previously thought that you would need to be impatient for.

Whenever I needed to get people to do what they didn't initially want to do, I automatically became impatient. Somehow I felt that by showing others that I was impatient they would rush. Looking objectively, I now realize that this had highly negative side effects. When I was impatient with my employees, they resented me. Some even tried to get back at me in passive aggressive ways. With my children, I caused them a lot of pain. And my impatience gave them a message that they weren't important enough to me to be more patient.

After I made the commitment to be patient even when I had to motivate others, I found patterns of speaking that made those I spoke to feel good and even more motivated than before to meet my requests.

FINDING A BALANCE

Sometimes people give patience a bad name. They waste their own time and the time of others and when this is pointed out to them they say, "You need to be more patient." Others have a tendency toward laziness and often procrastinate. When they are told to take care of things faster, they say, "You should be more patient."

I have heard some people say, "If we would be patient around here, we wouldn't get anything done."

Getting things done is one of the important things in the world. True patience that is a virtue is not a form of laziness and procrastination nor of wasting precious time. Rather, patience is a calm attitude toward situations that cannot be changed. Patience is freedom from muscle tension. It is manifested in one's body language, tone of voice, and patterns of speaking. Patience that is a virtue goes hand in hand with effectiveness and accomplishing.

We all need to find a balance between getting things done and using our time wisely and at the same time being patient with other people who are not as quick and efficient as we would like them to be. We need to be patient when delays beyond our control occur.

We need to find a balance between accepting things as they are and finding solutions that will improve a situation.

Every individual is unique and everyone's life situation is different. We each need to interact with different people. Two people may have an equal amount of internalized patience. Yet one is challenged constantly while the other is not. Therefore the precise meaning of being balanced will be uniquely your own. We are not offering an exact formula of how to create the perfect balance. But knowing that being balanced is important in this trait, just as it is in every other trait, gives us a general principle to be aware of that is conducive to creating a healthy balance.

I am always in a rush. I consider it my highest priority to get as many things accomplished as I can during my lifetime. I have met people who frequently sing the praises of patience. To me this is just their rationalization not to accomplish as much as they could.

What changed my attitude towards patience was an angry outburst of someone close to me.

"I can't keep up with you," I was told. "I feel a constant sense of pressure and tension when I am in your presence. No matter how fast I do things, I always feel that I need to do them faster to suit you. I can no longer tolerate your impatience. I've met high achievers who

are much calmer than you. Your impatience isn't healthy for you and it's not something that I want to live with."

I was ready to defend my need to accomplish. But this wasn't the real issue. I needed to find a proper balance. I was dedicated to create an inner sense of patience while using my time as wisely as I could. Even before I had reached my total goal, I was told, "You are so much more enjoyable to be around. I respect you for the way you have recreated yourself." This positive feedback showed me that I was on the right path.

EASIER SAID THAN DONE

A comment that I hear frequently is, "That's easier said than done." I always agree with this. Yes, it is much easier to talk about setting and reaching important goals than actually reaching them. Yes, it is much easier to talk about positive character traits than actually mastering them. Yes, it is much easier to talk about accessing the most positive, resourceful states than actually accessing them.

And the reason that it is easier said than done is that we need patience to actually develop positive qualities and master various skills. Talk is easy. Action is much more difficult. And when it comes to having the patience to do and become all that we can, it takes patience to develop this patience.

No reasonable person could ever claim that it is easy for someone who lacks patience to become a model of patience. "According to the difficulty is the reward," teach the Sages. The reward for mastering patience is immense.

Everyone can do that which is easy. It takes courage, determination, stamina, endurance, dedication, and consistent empowerment to do what is truly difficult. These also are qualities that take patience to develop. And that is why you can cherish every opportunity to become a more patient person. The gates to mastery of these life-enhancing attributes are open to those who excel in patience. Let them be open for you.

One of my favorite slogans used to be, "Easier said than done." I had heard this from an older person when I was a child, and it stuck with me.

An insightful mentor eventually told me, "When you comment that something is easier said than done, you are really stating an obvious truth. But you seem to use this as an excuse for not trying. From now on when you catch yourself saying this, immediately be resolved to have the patience and determination to make the necessary effort.

CLIMB ONE STEP AT A TIME

When climbing a high mountain, the general rule is: You need to climb one step at a time. You may look up at the summit of that mountain and wish to jump to the top in one major leap. But in reality that would never work. The only way to climb the mountain is one step at a time. Keep it up and you will reach your destination.

Those who become impatient never reach the top of the mountain. Their wishing for the impossible prevents them from spending the necessary time and effort to accomplish the possible but difficult.

We each have personal mountains to climb. Someone whose highest priority in life is to become a great scholar cannot do this overnight. It takes time to gain knowledge one page at a time. One who wants to become a great teacher or public speaker needs to master information and communication skills one class or lecture at a time. One who wants to gain deep understanding of other people needs to master the knowledge of one person at a time. One who wants to amass a financial fortune will find that the vast majority of get-rich-quick schemes do not work. He needs to make many intelligent decisions one at a time. One who wants to improve a complex difficult situation needs to solve it one step at a time.

When you have a long journey ahead of you, one step at a time does not seem as if it will get you as far as you want to go. But studying the lives of those who have gone the farthest teaches us that one step at a time is the pattern of those who have made it. When you travel in the right direction and consistently and continuously take one step at a time, eventually you will be able to look back at the distance you have traveled and will see the wisdom in having had the patience to take those multitudes of single steps.

I was over 30 and was extremely disappointed that I hadn't accomplished what I had thought I would ten years before. I was always told that having a sense of vision is crucial for great success. My sense of vision was magnificent but my accomplishments were way below what they could have been.

I consulted an older person with much experience. After asking me many questions, he said to me with compassion, "I see how important it is for you to accomplish many great things. That's highly commendable. What you are not yet doing right is that you are impatient to have things accomplished without taking a step-by-step approach. The only way to ensure that in ten years from now you will look back with a sense of fulfillment and satisfaction is to concentrate on one step at a time. I realize that for someone with your dreams and goals that sounds a little mundane and limiting. Nevertheless, that's the only way you'll make it."

I realized that he was right. What has helped me remember this is that whenever I need to walk a long distance, I tell myself, "When I take one step at a time, I will get to where I want to go." This has served as a lesson for me in all areas of my life.

51

TAKING IT PERSONALLY

Those who find it easy to be patient do not take it personally when someone keeps them waiting. Those who perceive being kept waiting as a personal affront are likely to become intensely impatient.

"If he or she considered me important and valuable, I wouldn't be kept waiting." This pattern of thought breeds resentment and irritation.

"If he or she cared enough about me, they would have taken care of the matter without me having to ask a second time." Thinking this way will have a negative effect on the way one repeats the request and how one will feel the entire time.

Some people take things personally in situations and circumstances that an objective observer would easily see is not at all an expression of a lack of respect or caring. The other person kept you waiting because of totally unforeseen circumstances or because things took longer than expected.

If you feel the reality is that with more respect or caring the other party would not have kept you waiting, discuss it with them. Do so with positive wording and the outcome in mind. Always remember: By treating other people with sincere respect and love, you are more likely to bring out their best.

The stronger your own sense of self-esteem, the less threatened you will be by another person's alleged slight. Ideally, you will not assume that an unintentional pattern was meant to belittle you. Even if the delay could have been avoided, your sense of your own intrinsic and infinite worth will never be shaken. You will then find it easier to maintain a centered and balanced state even in the face of someone else's lack of respect and consideration.

I used to consider it a point of personal honor to strongly protest if someone kept me waiting. I was told by an older relative that this was a sign of weakness and a lack of true self-respect. At first I argued that this came from inner strength.

"Those who truly feel personal value don't need to be validated in trivial and insignificant ways," my relative said. "You validate yourself the most when you elevate your character." Deep down I knew this was accurate and was resolved to live with this awareness.

IF SOMEONE FAILS TO SHOW UP FOR A MEETING

I f you have an appointment to meet someone, and that person does not show up, you can have a meeting with yourself. Whatever else you will accomplish with your meeting, you have the opportunity to develop the character trait of patience.

As soon as you begin to become distressed even to a small degree, announce to yourself, "I hereby declare this to be my patience-building meeting."

First of all, until you speak to him, you do not know the exact reason for his not being there. Maybe he has a valid excuse and maybe not. Wait and see. But do not fail to show up for your own meeting with yourself. When you realize your tremendous worth as a child of the Creator, you realize that while you are now meeting with someone different than you had originally planned, the replacement will be a highly valuable person.

I am grateful to the individual who failed to show up for a meeting that he had scheduled for this hour. Even though I needed to take a cab to be on time, I gained by writing this segment. If you gain from this piece, you too can be grateful that he could not come.

The head of a large company told me: My time is valuable. I tended to get furious at people who failed to show up for business meetings. When I was told to use this time for introspection and personal growth, I suddenly realized that I myself had been lax about showing up for these meetings with myself. This enabled me to gain from sporadic meetings that didn't take place, and to calmly think of the wisest approach for dealing with repeated offenders.

53

SEARCH FOR SOLUTIONS

Problems consistently arise in everyone's life. But not everyone handles them in the same way. Some whine and complain. Others become overwhelmed and depressed, while others become irritable and angry. There are many who view each problem that arises as a challenge through which to grow. They seek solutions and if they cannot find one themselves, they consult others for their input and suggestions. This is the pattern we all should follow.

When a solution is obvious and easy to implement, even those who are prone to impatience will be solution oriented. The less obvious a solution, the more patience it takes to think of one. The more difficult to implement, the greater the need for patience to make the necessary effort to do what needs to be done to solve the problem.

People who whine and complain need to develop the patience to focus on potential solutions. Similarly, when one's main focus is on finding a solution, one is less likely to become overwhelmed or angry.

Direct your thoughts toward the outcome you want. As you continue increasing your level of patience, you will have the patience to search for solutions no matter how elusive they appear to be at first.

A mother of nine children related: I grew up in a home where the emotional climate tended to be chaotic. When problems arose, blaming and accusations would fly back and forth. I became so used to this that I thought it was the normal way to react when difficulties arose. When I married, this was the pattern I was used to and therefore I reacted with emotional drama as soon as I faced a stressful occurrence. Fortunately, my spouse was solution oriented.

Whenever I overreacted, my spouse would patiently say, "Let's work together to find an acceptable solution." Little by little, I've integrated this focus on seeking solutions and the entire quality of my emotional well-being has greatly improved. My children are benefiting now by having a solution-oriented role model. I feel great pleasure when I reflect on how this will eventually have a positive effect on the lives of my grandchildren and great-grandchildren.

KEEP IMPROVING

Keep improving in all important areas in your life. Have the patience to continually ask yourself, "How can I do even better?"

When you already do well, it is easy to be complacent and satisfied. It takes patience to spend time thinking about how you can do even better. Those who do this consistently will excel. Develop the "How can I do even better?" habit and you too will excel in many areas.

A word of caution: To do this properly, feel a sense of pleasure with every bit of improvement. If someone were to keep thinking, "I never do good enough since there are always ways I can improve," he would experience constant frustration and stress. This counterproductive pattern is not conducive for bringing out one's best. Be grateful and appreciative for what you already do well and look forward to being even more grateful and appreciative as you make the effort to keep improving.

Which are the five areas of your life where you would gain the most if you consistently kept improving? By making patience and persistence one of those five areas, you will increase your level of improvement in more and more areas.

I was doing all right at my job. I enjoyed what I was doing, but didn't feel a deep sense of satisfaction. When I met people who were much more enthusiastic about their jobs, I wished that I could have similar excitement. I decided to find the key factors that made the difference. The pattern that I was determined to emulate was the constant drive to improve. In the past I had been too impatient to continuously work on constant improvement. But my realization that this would greatly upgrade the emotional quality of my life motivated me to keep asking myself, "How can I do even better?"

YOU NEVER KNOW
WHAT YOU MIGHT GAIN

When you have to wait for someone or something, you never know what and how you might gain. Keeping this in mind can save you from the frustration and anxiety of impatience.

If you were to miss a bus, plane, or train because a clerk did his job too slowly, you may never know if you were saved from a serious accident.

If through someone's neglect you wait at home longer than you expected, it is possible that you will receive a call which makes a valuable positive difference in your life.

If you had to stay in a certain store, office, or waiting area longer than you thought was necessary, perhaps you will gain an opportunity to do an act of kindness for someone. You may be able to provide needed information, advice, or help. This is an eternal gain that was made possible by your being the right person at the right place.

Ask yourself, "What would I need to gain to be patient right now?" Even the most impatient people in the world would act patiently if they knew that they would gain in some major way that is important to them. It always boils down to a matter of motivation. When you are motivated enough, you will have the ability to be patient.

There is always some gain in waiting. Some you will realize within a short time. In other instances, it might take a longer time until you can see the gain. By internalizing Rabbi Akiva's Talmudic principle, "Everything the Almighty does is for the good," you will realize that you always gain even though you are not yet aware exactly how that gain will manifest itself.

I had a friend who was badly injured when crossing the street against the light. He was impatient to wait for the light to change and this caused him much pain, and loss of time and money. From then on whenever I had to wait for a light to change, I focused on the gain of remaining in good health.

IF IT WERE EASY, IT WOULD HAVE BEEN DONE ALREADY.

I f solving a complex problem were easy, it would have been solved already. If enabling two people who have been quarreling for a long time to make peace and relate harmoniously were easy, it would have been done already. If motivating a nonmotivated child or a student were easy, he would have been motivated already. If overcoming our faults were easy, they would have been corrected already.

Patience is needed whenever finding a solution does not prove easy. This is not an easy world and therefore we need to master patience to master many other things. And if mastering patience were easy, everyone would already be patient.

If one expects something that is difficult to be much easier than it is, he is likely to experience high levels of frustration. Recognizing that something difficult is difficult does not make it easy, but it prevents making the difficult even more difficult.

My experience is that when it comes to self-development,

many people respond, "But that's very difficult." What they imply is, "This is too difficult for me so I am going to give up." They are partially right: mastering positive traits and states does take effort. We need the patience to persist and persevere. Repeating positive concepts and attitudes that we want to become a part of ourselves takes effort. Therefore we need the patience to repeat them enough times until we integrate them.

We do not need patience for what we find easy. By its very definition, patience is needed when things are not easy. It is exactly in these situations when you will experience the most pleasure by accomplishing something meaningful. And if it were easy, it would greatly diminish your accomplishment.

I have a friend who suffers from depression. He needs a lot of support and encouragement. At times I get discouraged. The efforts I put into cheering him up don't seem to have any lasting effect. I sometimes feel like giving up. What keeps me motivated are the words that my Rabbi told me, "Of course it's not easy to overcome a severe bout of depression. If it were, there wouldn't be so many people who are depressed. It's a great act of kindness to cheer this person up. When you give food to a poor person, he still needs another meal and another meal. The same is with emotional needs. Have the persistence to continue as long as this person needs you."

57

THE PATIENCE TO LEARN

"I don't have the patience to attend that class."
"I don't have enough patience to read that book."
"I'm too impatient to listen to that tape."

Schoolchildren are stuck. Whether or not they feel they have patience, they have to go to school, sit in the classroom, and read books. They can escape classes they find boring by mentally going elsewhere. The goal of each teacher is to stimulate the children sufficiently for them to concentrate on what is being taught. Some teachers do this by making the subject matter interesting. Others do this by pointing out, "This information may be useful on the next exam," while others do this by saying, "You'll lose your recess if you don't listen carefully." Of course, it is preferable if the teacher enjoys the subject matter and conveys this to the students.

Adults, however, have a greater degree of choice. The more motivated someone is to learn new things, the more patience he will have to attend lectures, read books, and listen to tapes.

If you lack the patience to learn new things, find ways to make the subjects more interesting for yourself. Clarify the benefits of knowing what you will be learning. The greater the benefits, the more patience we have. Think of ways you can apply what you learn. Imagine teaching the material to others. Do not only imagine this, find opportunities to share what you learn.

If you lack the patience to read an entire book, read a chapter or a few pages. If you lack the patience to listen to an entire tape, listen for ten or fifteen minutes or ask someone to summarize the key points for you.

I often said, "I don't have the patience to read this or hear that."

A friend challenged me, "You are losing out by not attending lectures or listening to tapes. You are making an assumption, 'I won't gain very much from this or that.' How do you know?"

That was exactly what I needed. I don't really know how much I'm losing. I am more motivated by fear of losing out than by imagining how much I would gain. I attended a number of lectures that previously I wouldn't have gone to. And I borrowed some educational tapes. It really hit me that I had lost out a lot. That is how I now motivate myself, "I don't want to lose out any more than I have already lost."

58

PATIENCE TO UNDERSTAND A TEXT

When you read something and it does not make sense to you at first, what is your initial reaction? Some people react, "This is too difficult for me. I give up." Those with patience react, "I'll read this a number of times until I understand it. If I need to, I'll come back to this text a while later to see if it's clearer to me in a day or two. If I can't figure it out myself, I'll consult someone who will be able to explain it to me."

At times when a text first appears to be too difficult, reading a more basic text on the subject can give us a foundation that will make the present text easier to understand. It can take patience to find out if there is such a text and where to get it.

Every time you read a text and find it more difficult to understand them you would have wished, develop the attitude, "Here is yet another opportunity to continue to develop more patience."

Recall a text that was too difficult for you the first time you read it, and later on you were able to comprehend it. This will demonstrate the fact that your initial difficulties with a text does not mean that you will not understand it eventually. When you think about this, you will realize that we all understood texts at the age of 10 that we could not understand at the age of 6. And at the age of 15 we were able to understand what we could not at the age of 10. Hopefully, you will continue to grow and even if you did not understand a specific text at the age of 50, you may understand it at the age of 55.

"This is too difficult for me." That was my theme song throughout my life. I used to give up too quickly. In school, I did poorly. And as an adult, I didn't continue my education the way I should have.

What changed my attitude was hearing a noted scholar say that when he was younger his brain was totally blocked. He was one of the slowest children in his class. But he would review texts over and over again until he understood them. Eventually he made an almost miraculous breakthrough.

UNDERSTANDING OTHER PEOPLE

M ake it a top priority to understand other people. Even if you do not understand the individuality of a specific person, you will be able to do many acts of kindness for that person. But when you do understand the uniqueness of someone, you will be able to do more to help that person in diverse ways. When you understand someone well, you will be able to give better advice and suggestions. When you understand someone well, you will be able to have a positive influence on that person's life.

People can be complex. There can be many reasons why a person does what he does and does not do what he should be doing. There are many traits and under various circumstances people will act in inconsistent ways. There are many emotions that an individual will experience. Each person has a unique life history and a unique genetic makeup. Each person perceives situations and occurrences differently.

Be patient when trying to understand another person. Some people are easier to understand, others are more difficult. Those who are similar to you will often be easier for you to understand. But patience is still necessary to recognize the differences.

The book *Gateway to Self-knowledge* lists over two hundred traits and thousands of questions to pinpoint patterns and their exceptions. The Introduction notes that if a person's personality would contain just twenty characteristics, each of which can be rated on a ten-point scale, over one hundred quadrillion different descriptions of people would be possible. No mortal can totally understand another human being. Only the Creator has total knowledge. But the more patient you are, the greater chance to gain a more accurate understanding.

Regardless of how well you understand another person, realize that there will always be new insights that you can gain. People constantly learn new things, have new experiences, and face new challenges. These create changes. At times these changes will be minor and at times major. So even if you feel that you already know someone well, have the patience to pinpoint distinctions you were not previously aware of.

I'm a black-and-white type of person. I tend to see things as either-or. There are the good people and the bad, the kind and the selfish, the intelligent and the stupid, those with positive characters and those with negative.

"You're intelligent enough to realize that there are an unlimited amount of nuances in each attribute and pattern," I was told. "What you lack is patience. Increase your level of patience and you will observe many new distinctions that you haven't noticed before."

In the past, just being told that I was either-or with a limited binary system didn't change my way of seeing people. Knowing that I needed patience gave me greater clarity as to what I needed to do.

TIME CONSTRAINTS

Even if someone has already made patience an integral part of his character, the limitations of time will create a need to rush. You have to meet an important deadline for a project. The plane will depart on its schedule, not yours. The Sabbath or holiday will soon be here and the amount of work left to do might appear to require a miracle to be completed on time. Guests will be arriving any minute and there are still many things to do. You assured someone that you would do something for him by a certain time and you are already late.

"Make haste slowly." This advice by Rabbi Noach Weinberg, founder and head of Aish Hatorah, will come in handy whenever you need to complete something by a certain time. True, you need to move quickly. But do so serenely. Your hands and feet need to move as fast as they can go. But your inner atmosphere can be serene.

When you are in a rush, there is no law that you need to create a panic state. Elevated levels of anxiety are not conducive to competent speed. An optimal state has been called a flow state. In your flow state, your brain is clear, focused, alert, and relaxed. In this state your brain works at lightening speed. Your hands and feet take action and are guided by your inner intuition about what needs to be done and how to do it. You feel great and concentrate totally on the task at hand.

Scholars who are totally absorbed in what they are studying are in this state. Professional athletes at their best are in this state. Writers and artists who are totally engaged in their creativity are in this state. Masters of any skill who focus entirely at the task at hand are in this state. And as you focus on accessing this state, you too will find yourself in a flow state when you are in a rush.

Remember a time in the past when you were in this state. Many young children who are totally focused on a toy with which they are playing will be in this state. Nothing else exists except what they are involved with. Look at their faces and see how they are totally absorbed in what they are doing. If someone calls them, they often do not hear those external sounds. Time goes quickly for there is no awareness of time. You were once a child and you must have been in this state before. If you can remember specific instances that occurred at any age, that's terrific. Then you are aware of the state you wish to increase now. If you cannot yet remember a specific time you were in this state, be aware of it after the next time you experience it. This will happen when you spontaneously become totally absorbed in what you are doing.

The type of work I am involved in is precisely the field I want. My biggest problem used to be that it consisted of one deadline after another. As soon as one project or task was completed, another deadline had to be achieved. I was in a constant state of stress. After a number of years, my health was greatly effected. A doctor warned me that my professional lifestyle was harmful to my heart and if I wanted to live to retirement age I had better slow down.

I was in shock when I was told this. I loved my work. At the same time I knew that the doctor was right. I remembered hearing about a flow state. I interviewed a number of people I knew who lived with constant deadlines which they consistently reached but seemed to be calm about it. Some of them admitted that they were more nervous and tense on the inside than it appeared on the outside and this did have negative psychosomatic effects.

A few of the people I spoke with described what I would call their flow state: total absorption full speed ahead. They were inwardly serene as they took action. I have made it a high priority to master the ability to access this state.

61

RUSHING PEOPLE GENTLY

People do not always proceed as quickly as we would want them to. Every married couple experiences this, every parent experiences this, every employer experiences this, every person who works with a group or team experiences this, every person who has to wait in a line experiences this. In short, the only way you will not experience this is if you live as a hermit all by yourself.

When you ask others to go faster, you have an option of how to word your message. There are words that engender bad feelings. And there are ways that are an expression of respect and sensitivity.

Let us discuss ways how not to speak to people:

> "What's taking you so long? You're so slow a turtle would go faster."

> "Hurry up! Hurry up! Hurry up! Get going!"

> "Move already or else!"

> "What's wrong with you! Have you lost your marbles?"

Imagine being on the receiving end of these statements. They are obviously painful.

Now let us discuss preferable patterns:

> "Pardon me, but I'm in a rush. Could you please go faster."
>
> "I would greatly appreciate your moving more quickly."
>
> "Ordinarily this speed is ideal. However, as I am late I must ask you to go as fast as you can right now."
>
> "I would be extremely grateful if you could do this quickly."
>
> "I'm sorry to inconvenience you. But I have a problem and need your help in solving it."

The question to keep asking yourself is: "What is the most sensitive and kindly way that I can word my request for speed?"

If you find yourself repeatedly having to rush people, it would be wise and compassionate to write down a list of about ten tactful ways to word your requests. Practice repeating those sentences over and over again until you find that you automatically say them even when you are in a rush.

When I was a child, my mother would say to me, "Come on, slow-poke. Don't go so slowly." I heard this so many times that it became a major part of my identity. Who was I? I was a slowpoke.

I married a wonderful person who believed in my ability to do things quickly. I had mentioned when we first met that I tend to do things slower than most people, and I was told that it didn't matter. What my spouse did for me was terrific. Every time I did something quickly, I was told, "I knew all along that you really are much faster than you thought." After hearing this enough times, my self-image changed. I now view myself as a person who can do things quickly and the actual time it takes me to do things is remarkably less than before.

62

READ AND FOLLOW INSTRUCTIONS

Failure to follow instructions can at best cause a lot of wasted time and at worst cause serious injury and could even be fatal. Those who are too impatient to carefully read instructions have to reinvent the wheel. When dealing with dangerous equipment, not reading or following instructions can cause harm to oneself and others.

Every time you read instructions even though your initial reaction is to skip it, you increase your level of patience. This alone makes it a worthwhile practice.

What if you read or hear instructions but do not totally understand them? Have the patience to read those instructions as many times as necessary or to ask for them to be repeated. Here there is a tendency for impatience and ego to add up together for a dangerous combination. It takes humility to acknowledge that one did not understand instructions that should have been understood. And it takes patience to spend the extra time reading or listening.

Generally, when someone is very excited about trying something new, reading the instructions is not high on the priority list. The more excited you are about increasing your level of patience, the easier it will be to overcome the temptation not to benefit from instructions.

I have a few close friends who excel at figuring things out on their own. Whenever possible, they take pride in not requiring someone else's instructions. But I have noticed that they have made avoidable mistakes. Somehow they discount the near misses that could have been serious. One sentence I have heard them say a number of times is, "I don't have the patience to read instructions." This is exactly what keeps motivating me to read instructions. I don't want to be a victim of impatience.

63

EMOTIONAL PAIN AND PATIENCE

Life presents each of us with emotional challenges. In everyone's life painful emotions will be at the forefront of one's consciousness from time to time. Patience enables you to bear distressful feelings until they are lifted and are replaced with more positive ones.

"This too shall pass." We have all heard this classic awareness many times. Without patience, one focuses on the pain of the moment. One might feel that the emotional pain will last forever. This can be overwhelming and cause discouragement.

With patience you know that tomorrow is just a day away. Similarly, a week, a month, and even a year will eventually arrive. When you realize that your distress is only temporary, you will be able to cope with it that much better. Patience enables you to think, "Have courage. This won't last."

There are many possibilities of what can happen to lighten our heavy spirits. A positive event or occurrence may occur.

We may gain a new spiritual awareness that will inspire and enlighten us. We may encounter someone who will tell us just what we need to hear to alleviate our pain. We may become so involved in a worthy project or kind act that the emotional pain dissipates. We may read something that will enable us to gain greater mastery over our emotional states. We may learn how to live totally in the present and view the pain of the past as part of our ongoing spiritual and emotional development. We may experience events and accomplishments that will give us a greater comprehensive perspective of what those times of distress actually mean to us.

"Be patient. This will pass." As time passes you will feel better. Let these words be an automatic part of your consciousness. Mentally hear these words loud and clear. Let these words resonate and permeate your being. And since you will feel better later, you may even choose to feel better right now.

I have an intense emotional nature. Irritants, insults, and setbacks that seem minor to others effect me strongly. Some people just try to metaphorically hit me over the head with a verbal hammer. "Grow up." "Don't be an idiot to allow such a trivial thing bother you." I've even been told, "You aren't normal. You have serious problems."

Someone who truly understood me and my emotional nature said to me, "What you need most is patience. You always overcome your emotional pain. Patience will enable you to realize that your distress won't last. And with patience, you will internalize the concepts and reframes that will enhance your emotional life. With patience you will learn and apply tools and techniques that will increase your positive emotions and decrease the negative ones."

He was right. After I made it a high priority to be more patient, the emotional quality of my life improved extraordinarily.

64

PATIENCE DURING PRAYER

Prayer is an exercise in increasing our patience. People who have a tendency to become impatient easily can be greatly challenged by different aspects of prayer. The greater one's emotional involvement in the meaning of prayer, the more absorbed one will be and the easier it will be to have the necessary patience. As you integrate the awareness that when you pray, you are talking to your Father, your King, Creator and Sustainer of the universe, the more absorbed you will be.

The ultimate goal to strive for is to be so immersed in the spirituality of praying that patience will not be an issue. In a number of my previous writings, I have cited from the Chazon Ish (*Emunah U'Bitachon* 1:9) the effects of awareness of the Almighty: "When a person merits becoming aware of the reality of the Almighty's existence, he will experience limitless joy. All the pleasures of the flesh immediately disappear. His soul is enveloped in sanctity and it is as if he has left the body and floats in the upper Heavens. When a person transcends to this level, an entirely new world is open to him. It is possible for a person to be momentarily like a celestial being in this world. All of the pleasures of this world are as nothing compared to the intense pleasure of a person cleaving to his Creator" (My Father, My King: Connecting with the Creator; ArtScroll/Mesorah, 1996).

While the above is an ideal to be aware of, every degree of concentration and mindfulness when we pray is precious. If you find that your mind wanders and that you are becoming impatient, calmly and gently bring your mind back to the present moment. Right now you are in the midst of prayer: focus on the words you say and to the One to Whom you are saying them.

The more patient you become, the higher your level of prayer will be. And the higher your level of prayer, the more patience that will be yours. This will have a beneficial effect on you throughout your day.

We will all have off days. We will all face situations that elicit our impatience. At times we will be in a rush to take care of something. That is when praying properly will have the greatest effect on our character.

As soon as I would begin praying, my mind would immediately focus on all the things that I had to take care of. This would create an impatience that could be quite intense at times. What helped me become more patient was the thought: "I am praying to the Almighty Who is the essence of patience."

THE FRUIT OF RUSHING IS REGRET

"The fruit of rushing is regret." This wisdom from *Mivchar Peninim* crystallizes the negative impact of impatience. The fruit of the apple tree is apples. You can eat the apples as they are or make delicious apple pie and applesauce. The fruit of the orange tree is oranges which can be eaten as is or which can be made into healthy orange juice. The fruit of the grapevine is grapes that are tasty themselves and from which you can make wine. All these fruit take time to grow. Rushing, however, speeds up the process. You might appear to save time. The problem is that in the overall large picture of life you lose more than you gain.

When you rush to speak or act without thinking, you will inevitably say and do things that you will regret. Will you always regret what you say and do when you rush? Not necessarily. But frequently you will, and the harm can be great.

Rushing without having the patience to think things through

carefully is like running in the wrong direction. You are going with speed. But the more quickly you go, the further away you are from where you really want to be. The time you appeared to save will be lost in what you will need to do to correct your mistakes.

I had to make a major financial decision. I was feeling a great amount of anxiety about this and wanted to get it over with as fast as possible. A close relative of mine kept telling me, "Take it easy. Go slow. Gather as much information as you can. Speak it over with a few experts."

"He doesn't know how anxious I feel," I said to myself. So I made a quick decision. The loss I incurred took me over five years to recoup. Spending an entire week on contemplating my best options would have saved me much time and suffering.

66

IMPATIENCE BEHIND THE WHEEL

Everyone knows that drinking and driving is dangerous. When a person drinks an alcoholic beverage, his judgment is distorted and his reflexes are less reliable. Often the person with high levels of alcohol in his system does not realize how strongly he has been effected. Driving after drinking has caused many serious car accidents. In every part of the world, law-enforcement officers ticket and fine those who risk their own lives and the lives of others by driving under the influence of alcohol.

Impatience when driving can be just as dangerous as alcohol. An impatient driver is likely to take risks that should not be taken. He may try to beat a racing train. Waiting while the train passes will take a few extra minutes. If the driver beats the train to the crossing, he saves three or four minutes. If the driver loses the race, it will mean his funeral and the funerals of his passengers.

An impatient driver will try to pass slower cars despite the rules of safe driving. An impatient driver will go faster than the speed limit. An impatient driver will drive across an intersection even after the light turns red. All of these practices and similar ones are like playing Russian roulette with a loaded gun. One time too many can be fatal.

Anyone who drives needs to learn to be patient. If there is anyone you care about who is an impatient driver, patiently and compassionately do all you can to motivate him to be patient, at least when driving."

I have a close relative who is highly impatient. I care about him a lot, but he considers me a nag when I tell him to be more patient when driving. I spoke the matter over with an older relative.

"Boycott him," I was advised. "Tell him that you refuse to go in his car until he is totally committed to be patient when driving."

My relative was very upset with me about this. I would regularly clip out articles about fatal car accidents caused by impatience. I felt tremendous relief when my relative told me one day, "You finally got your point across. I am committed to be patient whenever I drive."

67

PERCEPTIONS OF PATIENCE

Some people equate patience with passivity and weakness. Their mental image of someone who is consistently patient is a person who lacks inner strength. Their picture is incorrect. True patience that is a virtue goes together with mental toughness and an indomitable will. It is an inner strength that combines with kindness, compassion, and sensitivity. The ideal mixture will not happen simply by chance. It takes a conscious effort to create the optimal personality.

Someone who is not highly motivated, lacks assertiveness, fears the disapproval of others, and tends to be passive will act and react patiently. But this is not the ideal to strive for. Rather, patience is praiseworthy when someone is highly motivated to accomplish, can easily speak up and assert himself, has transcended all fear of disapproval, and tends to be proactive and still consistently speaks and acts patiently.

The stronger someone's basic personality, the more elevated that person is with highly developed patience. In my book Courage, I wrote about developing assertiveness. The more assertive you are able to be, the more important it is for you to develop patience. Yes, you have the ability to say whatever you feel like saying to another person. Therefore it is imperative to be patient with those who might be slow or inefficient. When you try to rush them or point out ways they can improve, do so with compassion and sensitivity.

I met someone who ran a boot camp. He dealt with tough juvenile delinquents. He told me that upon arrival no one could have described them as paragons of patience. They viewed being patient as being suckers and being wimpy but their lack of patience caused them to be aggressive and even violent. His goal was not to turn them into submissive personalities. Rather, he felt that he was successful when they transformed their roughness and toughness into strong personalities who had the self-discipline and self-mastery to be patient.

WHEN SOMEONE ATTEMPTS TO PROVOKE YOU

There are individuals who attempt to provoke you when they know that you are working on patience.

These are the type of people who get pleasure in seeing that others have faults. They feel better about themselves if they can prove that others are also not perfect.

While they are wrong in trying to point out your weakness, you can gain from their challenges. If you succeed in maintaining your patience, you can feel the joy of the positive feedback. If you become impatient with them, you can tell yourself, "Since my goal is to have this positive character trait, I can appreciate the feedback. I now know that I still have room for improvement. It's better to live in reality than to have an illusion."

The great Sage Hillel is our Talmudic model for mastery of patience in the face of provocation. In the renowned incident, one individual boasted that he could cause anyone to become angry. His friend argued, "No one can make Hillel angry."

The provocation consisted of going to Hillel's house Friday afternoon when Hillel was bathing in honor of Shabbos. The man asked irrelevant questions, in addition to calling out Hillel's name in a rude manner. Although it was a time when Hillel was in a great rush, he maintained calm patience each time the man returned with another questionable question.

The man seeing that Hillel was a paragon of patience, told him that he has many more questions to ask. Perhaps Hillel would tell him, "Enough is enough already." But Hillel surprised him by saying, "Feel free to ask all the questions you wish."

Only after seeing that Hillel had totally perfected this quality did the man concede that he is ready to give up trying.

The goal to emulate Hillel is a lofty one. I have often quoted my teacher, "When you reach for the stars, you might not catch any. But at least you won't get your hands stuck in the mud."

I was a member of a study group that was working on the trait of patience. There was an acquaintance of ours who was known for his cynicism. "If someone works on a trait, he will probably do worse than if he left things alone," he used to say.

He went out of his way to cause the members of the group to lose their cool. Little did he know that the experienced leader of the group had warned us of this possibility.

"The man who provoked Hillel made him great," he told us. "For many centuries the extent of Hillel's patience on that Friday afternoon has enabled a multitude of people to become more patient. View anyone who tries to provoke you as a teacher. And be grateful for the lessons you will learn."

PATIENCE IN A DIALOGUE

When two people disagree, it is common for each party to be impatient. Each one wants to change the other's opinion and perspective. Each one sees the facts differently and is impatient to straighten out the other's thinking. The problem is that since neither is paying attention to what the other is saying, there isn't any actual progress. Each of them can even be further away from reaching an agreement after his interaction.

Be patient when trying to convince someone of the validity and truth of your position. At times, the only way to get the other person to listen to you is to listen to him first. This can take a major effort on your part.

If you find yourself in a struggle over who has the right to speak first, focus on your actual goal. You want to be heard. You will achieve this faster by taking the longer route of listening first.

View your listening as another opportunity to increase your level of patience. View not listening to the other person as a guarantee that you will not be listened to. This will give you a stronger motivation to be patient while the other person speaks.

It is often the best strategy to say to someone, "I see that you feel a strong need for me to hear what you have to say. I, too, feel a strong need for you to hear what I have to say. I will listen without interruption until after you have finished speaking. And then I would like you to listen to me without interruption. Is this acceptable?" Most people will agree to this.

I have a fiery nature. I love to express my opinions and I do so passionately. Those who agree with my views enjoy the way I speak. Unfortunately, I have been involved in innumerable shouting matches.

Someone finally shouted at me in anger, "Your problem is that you arrogantly don't want to hear what anyone has to say."

"But I'm not arrogant," I defended myself.

"You certainly act as if you are," I was told.

I tried to introspect objectively. I do have a basic respect for other people's opinions. And if I'm wrong, I'll admit it. I realize that I might be making a mistake. "So why don't I give others a fair opportunity to express themselves?" I asked myself.

"You're impatient," I heard my inner voice tell me. That rang true to me. I needed to develop greater patience when it comes to hearing what others have to say. Knowing what quality I needed to develop made it possible for me to work on improvement.

COPING WITH UNCERTAINTY

"**T**here is no greater joy than resolving doubts." In this often quoted aphorism we find that uncertainty is highly distressful. It causes so much anxiety that one of the greatest joys of life is to be free from its pain. Since uncertainty is an integral part of everyone's life, the ability to cope well with it is crucial for living a life of joy and inner peace.

Patience is serenity. When one masters patience, one has a higher level of tolerance for uncertainty. Achieving certainty in many areas takes time. Will I be accepted to the school I wish to attend? Will my business or project succeed? What will be the outcome of the election? What will be the results of the medical tests? How will things turn out in a multitude of areas?

Every uncertain situation is yet another opportunity to help you increase your patience. Transforming uncertainty into patience means that when you master patience, uncertainty will no longer be considered a problem. Rather, it is an integral part of your lifetime course on gaining patience. Dealing with uncertainty can be highly challenging. And that is precisely why it is so important to learn to cope with it.

I met a righteous Torah scholar who was always calm. He was the personification of an alert mind and relaxed body. I asked him how he remains serene when most people are nervous and full of anxiety when facing uncertainty.

"I am never uncertain," he said with a smile.

"Do you mean to say that you always know how things will turn out?" I asked incredulously.

"I do and I don't," he replied. "I don't know the exact details of what will be, just like everyone else. But I do know for certain that whatever will be will be according to the will of the Creator. Since I'm certain that whatever He does is for the good, I don't worry about what will happen."

PATIENCE AND PURCHASES

Many people do not feel the financial necessity to be as economical as possible. Others do, yet still do not research where to obtain the best deals. Why not? They tend to be impatient. Once they have decided to buy something, they are not patient enough to make the appropriate inquiries.

Patience can pay off financially. When you are informed of the difference in prices for similar commodities, you will know where to go for the best deal. You can even negotiate with those who originally quoted a higher price. This is not for everyone. But do not allow impatience to pressure you into an unnecessary loss.

Time is precious; more precious than money. So you may decide that it is worthwhile to pay more rather than to invest time into saving money. But if someone is dependent on the largesse of others for financial support, he owes it to them to decrease expenses. If someone is in debt and delays paying what he owes, he has an obligation to spend less to eventually clear the debt. If someone could give more to charity by spending less, he owes it to those he could help to spend less so he can provide more for them.

Learn from the experts. Some people regularly compare prices and quality before making a purchase. They take pleasure in saving money. If you would like to enjoy this also, ask them for their attitudes and thoughts on the subject. As you find out how they have the patience to do their research, it will help you acquire some of that patience also.

In the home where I grew up, we always had enough money to buy whatever we needed. My father had a well-paying job. He was short on time and it was easier for him to spend more and save time. I, however, had to live on a tight budget. I needed to make a major purchase and did so in the first store I entered. A day later I found out that I could have readily bought it for much less than I paid. My impatience got me into a debt that took a while for me to pay off. The benefit, however, was that I was resolved to consistently have the patience to do more research before any major purchase.

72

IMPATIENCE WITH INJUSTICE

It is proper to be impatient with injustice. When you need to correct someone who is open and rational, just pointing out the facts can be sufficient. The person will readily concede and acknowledge the mistake and will do all he can to correct the wrong. But when a closed and irrational person is committing an injustice, and a calm approach is not effective, you might find it beneficial to verbalize your impatience.

Always begin with respect and understanding. If the other party unjustly refuses to refund the money that is yours or even to apologize, your reacting with the intensity of anger can help you right the wrong. Save this for extreme situations. Compassion is powerful. Speaking with centered strength and determination will usually enable you to accomplish what you need to accomplish. But if you have tried calm options and they fail to help you achieve the outcome you are striving for, try being strategically impatient.

When people know that you are usually patient and are impatient only in emergencies, they are more likely to take what you say seriously.

Those who are frequently impatient should not use this idea as a rationalization to condone an impatient approach as a general way of being. But used wisely and discriminately, impatience has its time and place.

I have a friend who is an expert at writing letters of complaint. When he is overcharged, the extra money is usually refunded. When someone was disrespectful or rude, he usually obtains an apology. I asked him how he does it.

"I feel that I don't have a right not to complain. I need to defend other people who also might be treated unjustly. My first letter is always written with total respect and judging favorably. This is the way we should interact with everyone because it is intrinsically the right way to treat people. If this proves effective, then the matter is finished. If not, however, I write another letter stating a deadline for the wronged to be right. My tone is that of someone who means business. I use impatience strategically and find it highly beneficial."

73

CURIOSITY

The more curious someone is, the less patient he is likely to be about finding out information. At times we should strive to overcome our curiosity in its entirety to avoid causing others needless distress. People have a right to privacy and we should respect their wishes and their dignity. At other times, our curiosity can be appropriate, but we should exercise patience by wisely timing our request.

Curiosity can be a very positive quality. Curiosity can motivate a person to gain knowledge and information in important areas. What one is curious about reveals a lot about his personality and character. It would be considered a fault not to be curious about gaining wisdom and deeper understanding of important matters. But when curiosity is petty, it is most often a highly counterproductive tendency.

Some people are pleased to respond to your questions. If you would like to know something and they have the information, they are pleased to share what they know with you. Others are open to tell you things but only when they feel ready to do so. If you are impatient, your impatience may put pressure on them. So it is important to learn to read the nonverbal feedback (i.e. body language) of others when you ask them questions solely out of curiosity. Be sensitive to the wishes of others. Gain awareness of what they feel comfortable sharing with you and what they would prefer that you do not ask. If in doubt, ask them if they would prefer that you refrain from asking questions right now.

I tend to be an open person and usually don't mind when people ask personal questions. I am curious about others and feel that just as I am willing to answer questions about myself, others will be equally willing to tell me about themselves. Not too long ago, however, someone blew up at me.

"I can't stand how impatient you are to find out information," he told me. "It's none of your business to know information before others are prepared to tell you."

I hadn't looked at myself as an impatient person. I don't get angry at others very often and therefore I assumed that I don't have a problem with impatience. But I had to agree. I was impatient about finding out trivial information. Since that outburst I have been much more careful about asking curious questions. I now look at the need to wait to find out the latest news as my personal training in becoming more patient.

74

PATIENCE WITH THE VERBOSE

Some people might communicate in ways that are excessively wordy for you. When trying to give you a picture of a situation, they include numerous irrelevant details. You want to hear what they have to say, but would find it much easier to listen if they would be concise. You have a number of options.

At times you may view this as a patience workshop. The more detail they go into, the more patient you work at becoming.

At times, you may summarize the key points. This way they know that they have been heard. This will decrease their need to go on and on. This is especially important when someone is telling you about something he found very painful. He wants his feelings to be validated. You may say, "That must have been very painful." Or, "I can see that this was difficult for you."

At times, you may say, "I can get a clearer picture with fewer details. If I need additional details to make the picture clearer, I'll ask you questions. Is that acceptable to you?"

At times, you might be of great long-term help to this person by pointing out that he would gain by being more concise. He should clarify what outcome he is aiming for. And he should word his communications accordingly. Be careful how you suggest this. If it is not phrased properly, the person might be hurt and offended. When you have chosen the right words, the person will gain and will be grateful.

When I was younger, I heard a story about a great Torah scholar who was well known for his total devotion to his studies. He was a master at time management and used his time wisely. Yet he would listen carefully when someone who was in emotional pain would speak at much greater length than seemed necessary. He was asked about why he did this.

"I don't have a great deal of money to give to charity," he replied. "The biggest kindness I can do for some people who suffer is to be a compassionate listener. My listening is how I emulate the Almighty in being compassionate."

75

POTENTIAL FOR CREATIVITY

E veryone is creative. Some people already realize that they are. Others have not yet become aware of their potential for creativity. Patience enhances creativity.

Even the most creative people in the world will find themselves blocked at times. They will try to think of a creative solution to a problem or a creative idea in their profession or a creative thought for a speech or a class. And nothing happens. The creative idea does not pop into their consciousness. What they need is patience.

People who view themselves as noncreative need to remember that every young child is creative. Watch any child playing with building blocks, dolls, little cars and trucks, and other toys. Every single one will find a creative way to play with them. But we find that as adults those who believe that they are not creative will invariably have their beliefs validated. The first step in creativity is to believe that you have creative potential. Each person is creative uniquely. The way to access your creativity is through patience.

If you dream when you sleep, you are creative. And everyone dreams. Some people remember their dreams clearly and others have not yet developed this skill. For those who consider themselves uncreative, it could be worthwhile to make the effort to remember as many details of dreams as possible. Write them down. Be patient. Even if you have tried to remember a segment of any dream and thus far you cannot recall anything, when you patiently work on this overtime, you will make progress. Just telling your brain calmly before you fall asleep, "Tomorrow I will recall my dreams," will increase your brain's ability to remember your creative dreams.

Patiently brainstorm. If you are working on solving a problem, generate many possible solutions. When you are brainstorming, do not evaluate whether a potential solution is practical. Your goal is to get your brain to think of creative possibilities.

I used to envy people who were creative. "I'm not creative," I would say. I mentioned this to one of the most creative people that I know.

"If you were creative, what would you like to accomplish with your creativity?" he asked me.

"I would feel more intelligent. In general my entire self-image would be enhanced. I would feel more secure about getting a better job. I would have more enjoyment in life. My creativity would help me overcome boredom. I would have a better time when interacting with other people."

"Are you quoting this list from a specific source or did you hear it from someone?" he asked.

"No," I replied. "These are just the thoughts that came to mind."

"Well, then you are creative," he said with a smile. "Any time you say something that hasn't been said exactly that way before, you are being creative. A valuable key to creativity is to be patient. Every day take a blank piece of paper and let your thoughts flow. Write down some of those thoughts. Be patient enough not to stop writing until you finish an entire sheet of paper. Remember that your initial goal is not to write a masterpiece or to come up with a brand-new concept that will transform civilization. Your goal is to prove to your own self that you are more creative than you thought."

This approach helped me in two ways. I now view myself as being creative even though I thought that I never would. I have also become more patient in more areas of my life.

ASSERT YOURSELF RESPECTFULLY

There are people who passively remain quiet and do not ask for what they want. Then they become impatient. Speak up and ask for what you want, but do so politely and respectfully.

Some people fail to ask others for what they want because they are generally unassertive. They would like to speak up, but are too intimidated to do so. Inwardly, however, they feel resentful that they are not receiving better service. Their impatience simmers within and they suffer quietly. They need to increase their level of courage and should practice being more assertive. They can mentally visualize themselves speaking up in a self-respecting and respectful manner. Every act of assertiveness makes it easier to be more assertive in the future.

There are people who can easily be assertive, but they do not want to bother others. If they inwardly feel patient when waiting, this can be a highly commendable pattern. It is a conscious choice to go out of one's way not to be a burden on someone else. But if someone inwardly feels impatient and resentful, it is preferable to speak up and ask for what one wants.

My husband tends to procrastinate and doesn't take care of things right away. In the beginning of our marriage I would experience much impatience, but I wanted harmony and would push off reminding him for as long as I could. But after a couple of years I realized that my resentment caused me to get back at him in numerous passive-aggressive ways. I decided to speak up in an upbeat way whenever something was needlessly being pushed off. My husband appreciated the way I reminded him and we both gained a lot. Knowing that whenever I really needed something to be taken care of, I could speak up in a way that I would get results has enabled me to be a lot more patient.

I used to suffer in silence. I grew up in a home where we were frequently told, "Don't bother other people." So I went out of my way not to bother others. But waiting until someone would volunteer to help me caused me suffering from the distress of impatience. I spoke to an elderly scholar who told me that I needed to develop a more balanced approach to asking others for help. In effect I was depriving others from doing acts of kindness. While I kept my requests to a minimum, this was sufficient to save me from much distressful impatience.

HIS TIME IS ALSO IMPORTANT

Do all you can to avoid testing the patience of other people. Be sensitive to their time needs and concerns. When they are in a rush, do not needlessly delay them.

When you want to speak to someone and get a feeling that this person might not have enough time right now, ask, "Is now a good time for you?" Even if they say, "Yes," keep to the point and be careful not to take up more time than necessary.

When speaking to someone who is generally impatient, be as concise as possible. Mentally prepare in advance what you will say. In certain situations, it would be worthwhile to write what you plan to say on paper. You might want to begin by saying, "I'll be as concise as I can. Please be patient with me."

When you see that someone is busy and does not have much time, but the matter you wish to discuss is urgent or pressing on you, begin by saying, "I see that you are busy, and I respect that. What I need to talk to you about is important for me.

I would greatly appreciate your kindness." By acknowledging that this person is busy, you make it easier for him to be patient.

For a while I had a feeling that my fellow students would become more impatient and irritable with me than with others. I wasn't certain if this was actually the case or whether I just noticed it more when I was involved.

I approached an older student who was an expert in getting along with others.

"Please be straight with me, " I said. "Do I cause others to be impatient more than average?"

"I'm glad you approached me," he said. "I've wanted to speak to you about this. You seem to be oblivious to the emotional state of others. Most people realize when others are in a rush. You often stop people even though it's quite obvious that this person is in a hurry.

I realized he was right and I felt bad. I was highly motivated to develop a sensitivity to the time constraints of others. Being aware of this pattern enabled me to improve greatly in a short time.

DON'T BE AFRAID TO ASK

I f you are concerned that people might not be as patient with you as you would wish, ask them in advance for their patience.

You might say things like,

"Please be patient with me."

"I would greatly appreciate your patience."

"I work best when people I deal with are patient."

"I'm not as fast as I would want to be. And I realize that I'm not as fast you would want me to be."

"You look like a patient person. Please prove that I am right."

It has been found that it is often beneficial to start off a request with the words, "I have a problem, and I hope that you will be able to help me." Most people enjoy solving the problems of others when they are able to. Your turning to this person is a vote of confidence in his talents and abilities. After beginning by stating that you have a problem, you can say, "I don't understand instructions when they are said quickly.

Could you please say them slowly?" You might even want to add, "I see that you have been blessed with the speed that I would have wanted."

If you think that you might have to keep people waiting, tell them in advance, "I'm really sorry that I might keep you waiting. I am grateful for your patience."

At times you might find it helpful to say, "I have a problem. I'm afraid that you might become impatient with me." Even after you say this, the person might become impatient. But he is likely to be more patient than if you would not have said this.

If we have had the experience of being told to be patient and it was said to us in ways that we found distressful, those patterns might have become our own. If you ever remember having been told to be patient in a way that you did not like, tune in if you yourself ever talk like this to others. It might take a special effort to be careful not to repeat these patterns. Replace distressful patterns with pleasant ones. Then the people you communicate with will learn from your positive patterns and pass them on to others who also will pass them on. Thus you will be creating a positive chain.

My entire life I was apprehensive lest people not be patient with me. This was especially so when I had to ask for information on the phone. Face-to-face, I could tell if he was or wasn't going to be patient. Also, in person I could just stay there until I received the information

I needed. But on the phone I always had the feeling, "This person will just rattle off the information. I won't be able to follow him and he will hang up before I am able to clarify what I needed to know."

I kept looking for solutions. Finally I came across the idea of asking for patience in advance. This way I knew that I did all that I could. And I found that people tended to be more patient when they were explicitly asked for it in advance.

I used to go around telling other people to be more patient. I would say, "Why can't you be more patient?" and, "Your impatience is very rude."

This elicited negative reactions. I would blame the impatient people for not being more open to criticism.

Someone once witnessed me lambasting an impatient person. He approached me with sensitivity and said, "I, too, don't like it when others are impatient with me. I have found that the way I word my requests makes a major difference. Be compassionate toward the impatient. Their impatience causes them a lot of suffering."

I hadn't viewed it this way before. I began to see the distress of those who were impatient and this made it much easier for me to be more patient with them.

"THANK YOU FOR YOUR PATIENCE."

Reinforce the patience of others. Whenever someone waits patiently for you or answers your questions patiently, thank him. When you see that someone is patient when interacting with another person, express your appreciation for that patience. You might say something like, "I noticed how patient you were. I respect that."

When you give people feedback that their patience was observed and appreciated, they are more likely to be patient in the future. Your focusing on their having this quality reinforces it in their minds. Your positive feedback is creating more patience on our planet.

If someone tends to be impatient, the best way to help him increase his level of patience is to point out times and moments when he manifests patience. This is usually more effective than telling him, "I've seen your impatience. You need to change."

If you have been patiently reading this book from the beginning to this section, I want to commend you on your patience.

A group of employees who worked for someone who was frequently impatient decided to work together to effect a change. In the past a few of them had tried to tell the boss that he lost out a lot by being impatient. They meant well, but they were never successful. Sometimes the boss would either argue with them, "I'm more patient than you realize." At other times the boss would say, "The way I am is the way I am. And everyone else will just have to get used to it."

The new plan was to look for every instance of even minimal patience and to thank him profusely for it. They kept this up for over a month and to the surprise of everyone involved it was remarkably effective.

A COMMERCIAL CONCEPT

"Talking to this person is like talking to the wall. He doesn't argue, but my words don't even begin to have the positive effect I would want them to have."

When you feel that a concept, principle, or idea is important for someone, be patient. Most people do not hear something just once and immediately integrate it and make it their own reality. Be prepared to repeat concepts, principles, and ideas over time.

Learn from professional commercials. Companies and organizations that want to impress an idea in people's minds know that mental conditioning takes repetition. Every time you repeat a valuable idea to a child, a student, and anyone else you care about, realize that you are consistently making progress. But the way you word your message is vitally important.

Use positive wording. Be concise. And speak in a pleasant tone of voice.

Parents who want their children to be polite and respectful may need to repeat these messages hundreds of times. Telling a child, "You have no respect for your parents," is sending them a powerful message. If a parent wants his child to lack respect in the future, this is the way to do it. Parents who want their children to have respect would be wise to word their message, "It's important to speak and act respectfully. Do this and you have a valuable resource for your entire life." Each "commercial" will even be more effective if this is said in a soft, pleasant tone of voice.

Teachers should be aware of the main messages they want students to integrate. These messages should be worded concisely and repeated time and again. Use the wording of the Sages in Ethics of the Fathers as a model. Each concept can be elaborated on. But the basic concise message is what you want them to integrate. Each "commercial" adds to the depth of the impression.

Condition your brain to master patience. Repeat messages to yourself such as, "Patiently master patience."

"Enjoy the process of mastering patience."

"Rejoice with every patient victory."

"Every act of patience makes you a more patient person."

81

"YOU'VE NEVER..."

We will all find ourselves in situations when we need to help someone else become more patient. Some people easily access a patient state when you remind them to do so. All you need to say to them is, "Please access a patient state right now." They respond, "Thanks for reminding me." They then transform their present state from impatience to patience.

Many others have not yet mastered this skill. If someone finds it difficult to access patience at will, telling him in an angry voice, "Be more patient already," is not the most effective approach to help them access patience. If anyone has ever tried this with you, you will readily understand the problem with this pattern.

What you want to do is get an impatient person into a more patient state. You may be able to do this by reassuring him that the matter will be taken care of shortly. But this is not always realistic or even possible. Then you might want to try a polarity approach.

"You've never been patient before?" asked in a tone of voice expressing curiosity often elicits a response, "Of course, I've been patient many times."

Then you can ask for some specific instances. "What were some of the specific situations when you were patient?" Follow this by asking, "How exactly did you do it?" This helps a person recall past memories of patience which makes it more conducive to be patient in the present.

A word of caution: Some people strongly dislike polarity approaches, while others find them beneficial. Observe reactions and do not use this with those who find it irritating.

If you are someone who has a difficult time remembering your moments of patience, let me ask you now: "You've never been patient?" Hopefully, you will resent the question and will respond, "Of course, I've been patient many times." As you keep those memories in mind, you will find yourself adding to them.

82

PATIENCE ON THE JOB

Anyone in a management position at work affects the emotional climate of those he or she manages. This is true of businesses, schools, hospitals, and all other organizations. Your level of patience will have an impact on everyone you interact with.

In business, you want to make money, accomplish as much as possible, and keep to a schedule. Continually developing your character as you engage in these goals adds a spiritual dimension to all that you do.

Schools are intended to educate. Educate all those you manage to have patience under pressure. You educate best when you educate by your example.

Those who work in all areas of the health industry decrease stress and maximize healing by evidencing calm, soothing patience. In times of emergency, speed is of the essence. Speaking with respect to others should be such an integral part of one's being that even though one is in a supreme rush, the way one speaks reflects respect.

Speak with respect and patience to employees, co-workers, customers, and clients. It is easy to do so with your most valued customers and clients. You elevate your character the most by speaking respectfully to those who need you more than you need them.

The head of a large company told me: I have a successful business. I am generous with my employees and I donate large sums to many charities. But since I've always wanted to accomplish as much as I can, I used to be impatient with those who work for me.

As soon as I arrived at my office, I was bombarded with demands for my attention and time.

"Just give me the bottom line," was what I would frequently say. The tone of voice I used would make everyone feel uncomfortable.

My Rabbi told me that I needed to focus on one thing at a time. It was suggested that I sit in my chair for sixty seconds and access a patient state. I would make a daily resolution to speak patiently and respectfully to everyone.

I practiced saying statements such as:

"I believe in your intelligence. Please give me your bottom line suggestion."

"I would like to talk to you, and I will after I make this important call."

"I want you to know how valuable you are to the company. As soon as possible, I'll get back to you."

I now begin meetings by saying, "I want to save everyone's time. Please make each point concisely."

I found it amazing how effective the daily resolution was together with being prepared with patterns of respect.

83

WHEN THEY DON'T FOLLOW THROUGH

"**D**on't worry. I'll take care of it," someone tells you. But he doesn't. If this happens just once, you might easily assume that something unforeseen happened to prevent this person from doing what he said he would. But what if someone does this over and over again? How do you remain patient?

Gain an understanding of the underlying factors behind the person's pattern. Some people really intend to do what they say they will. But they find it difficult to refuse requests. They take on more than they can actually accomplish.

When dealing with this pattern, ask the person to be honest with you. You might say, "If this is too difficult and you can't do it, I'll understand. I want you to say yes only if you plan to actually do it."

Pay attention. The person might hem and haw and say something like, "Well, I'll see how it goes. I'll try if I'm not too busy." Take this as a message that he is probably not going to do it.

If the person who does not follow through is someone who has an obligation to do so, focus on the outcome you want. Find positive ways to motivate this person. Give him high doses of positive reinforcement when he does facilitate matters. Be encouraging in an upbeat tone of voice while wording what you say in a manner that expresses your belief in this person's abilities and a deep-down wish to be reliable. This can go a long way to produce the results you are hoping for.

I have a managerial position in a large business. We have a schedule to keep. Falling behind creates a problematic chain reaction. I used to blow up at people who didn't do what they said they would. Turnover in our department was high.

Finally, one brave new employee said to me, "I used to work for an even larger company. The owner was one of the most patient people I've ever met. I asked him how he remained so patient. He explained that working on his character was a higher priority than making more money. In reality, people appreciated him so much that they put in a great effort not to disappoint him."

This was helpful to me. While it took much effort for me to develop this outlook, I saw the benefits in a very short time.

84

WAITING FOR THE FLOOR TO DRY

Floors need to be cleaned. And it will take time for a floor to dry. While waiting for the water to turn into vapor, you have a choice: to be patient or not to be patient. View this time as an opportunity to increase your level of patience.

Appreciate the fact that water evaporates. This saves you time and energy. You do not have to strain yourself to mop up every last drop of water. You can wait for the water to transform itself into its new form. The evaporation of water is a miraculous process that creates the rain that waters trees, plants, and all forms of vegetation.

If someone else has washed the floor, be grateful for the work that person put into the job. Instead of being impatient for the waiting, be appreciative.

If you yourself have washed a floor and are impatient for the water to dry, imagine how difficult your life would be if you would not have water available. Be grateful that you have water. The fact that you have enough water to wash the floor is a reminder that you have enough water to drink.

In the blessing we make when drinking water we acknowledge the King of the universe Who has created all that exists through His will. Contemplating this while you are waiting for floors to dry will enhance your life spiritually and emotionally.

I once slipped on a wet floor and it was an amazing experience. As I was falling, time subjectively slowed down. Everything went into slow motion. It seemed to me that it took at least ten seconds for me to land. Someone who was near me at the time said that in actuality it was only a fraction of a second. What had happened was that my mind went into an altered state and my perception of time gave me a greater awareness than usual. Since then when I gaze at wet floors I remember that experience. It now serves as a reminder that my perceptions are subjective and I have the ability to find more comprehensive spiritual perspectives in what could otherwise be considered mundane. As it has been said, "To the truly spiritual, nothing is mundane."

STUBBORN PEOPLE
AS COACHES

Flexible people are easy to deal with. It does not involve a great deal of patience to interact with someone who is consistently reasonable, who understands your issues, is willing to compromise and work out a win-win solution.

Stubborn people, however, can be challenging. You need to repeat yourself. You need to offer alternative approaches. You need to spend time on understanding the real underlying issues behind their positions. You need to develop creative methods for moving them.

View a stubborn person as your patience coach. Every stubborn person you interact with properly will make you a more patient person.

Stubborn people are your partners in elevating your character. Having a more positive view of a stubborn person might not suddenly transform him. But it will be part of the process that little by little will transform you.

I used to hate stubborn people. They frustrated me beyond words. I became so uptight around them that as soon as I felt that someone was stubborn, my state immediately changed into an unresourceful one. My own impatience made them even more difficult to deal with.

The turning point for me was my beginning to view individuals who were stubborn as my personal trainers for becoming a master of patience. As soon as I realized that someone was stubborn, I heard an inner voice saying, "What a great opportunity to develop even greater patience."

My own reframe had a positive effect on how I acted and how they reacted. At times I even look forward to my next encounter with someone who is stubborn.

86

"YOU'RE RIGHT"

No matter how much you work on becoming more patient, you will nevertheless not be patient enough for some people. Agree with people who claim you need to be more patient.

Suppose you have been working on increasing your level of patience for a long time. You conquered your impatience over and over again. Then someone who is going much too slow says to you, "You need more patience."

One's initial reaction is likely to be defensive. "I am so much more patient than I used to be. I've put in a lot of work. It's wrong of you to tell me that I'm not patient enough."

There is never an amount of patience that is too much. So if you are challenged, "You need more patience," the proper response would be, "You're right. I do need more patience."

By acknowledging the need for more patience, you are opening yourself up for further improvement. This does not negate the effort you have already put in. But we can all gain even more patience regardless of the amount of patience we already have. These encounters enable you to maintain humility. No matter how much you have accomplished, when it comes to character development, there is always more to do.

Mentally practice.Visualize yourself in situations that will greatly challenge your ability to maintain patience. See someone telling you that you need more patience. Then either say out loud, "You are right. Thank you." Or you can mentally visualize yourself saying this. Run through this scene in your mind over and over again until you feel comfortable that you will be able to say this when the need arises.

Like most people, I find it distressful to be criticized. I would love to reach the level of appreciating criticism, but so far I am just on the beginning of this path. I've worked on patience and it's important for me to have this acknowledged. But the reality is that certain people in my life know that I still lack patience and they are quick to point this out to me.

"That's not fair," I would say irritably. "You have to admit that I'm more patient now then ever."

"But you still have a long way to go," they would argue.

I decided to overcome my defensiveness and acknowledge the truth of their claims. The next time I was told that I was impatient, I responded, "You are right. I still need to gain more patience. I'm working on it and my goal is to be much more patient than I presently am."

What was amazing to me was that when I said this, I was told, "I have noticed that you are more patient than you used to be. It's admirable that you have changed for the better."

87

ASK FOR FEEDBACK

Someone who is highly committed to overcome impatience will ask others for feedback. You may tell family and friends, "If you ever see me being impatient, please point it out to me."

If you ask for feedback, watch out for the tendency to argue with the person who tells you that you are impatient. It's easy to say, "I wasn't really impatient, I was just raising my voice a little," or, "What I meant by impatient is that I totally lose myself. I was still under control."

If you argue with people who try to help you overcome your impatience, they may be reluctant to get into discussions with you. So even if you feel that you were not actually impatient and someone gives you feedback that you were, thank them. "It was kind of you to point this out to me. Thank you for your concern." Some people find this relatively easy to say. If you would find it difficult, practice repeating this sentence: "It was kind of you to point this out to me. Thank you for your concern." How many times should you repeat this? As many times as necessary for you to feel so comfortable about saying this that it will feel totally natural.

Some people become defensive with the feedback of others. They might say things like, "It wasn't my fault I was impatient. This was taking a very long time." Or, "Anyone would be impatient in such a situation." It could very well be that it wasn't your fault and that anyone else would react the same way that you did. Nevertheless you did react impatiently. So the feedback can be acknowledged. The skill of expressing appreciation for feedback nondefensively is a great one to acquire. Take pleasure in developing this skill and that will enable you to transcend any distress you might otherwise have felt.

I used to be hypersensitive to criticism. If someone reprimanded me or pointed out that I did something wrong, I would obsess about this for an exceedingly long time. I remember the day I said to myself, "I am now making it my goal to be open to the constructive feedback of others. I will look at my willingness to weigh the feedback objectively as a strength that will be beneficial in many areas of my life. I am still not perfect in this, but I have made great progress. Now instead of just saying, "No one likes to be criticized," I say to myself, "I am gaining greater proficiency at the ability to appreciate opportunities for further personal development."

SLEEP, HUNGER, AND NUTRITION

When we are well rested, we tend to be more patient. When we are tired, we need to make a special effort to remain patient.

When we are hungry, it is easier to be impatient. After we have eaten properly, we become calmer. Even before you eat that food, watch what you say and how you say it.

Coffee, white sugar, chocolate, and various food allergies can have a major effect on one's level of tolerance or impatience. Gain awareness of your unique patterns. Knowing what to avoid will help you become more patient.

When I'm tired I easily become frustrated. I used to look at my impatience when I lacked sleep as inevitable.

I visited a couple with a large family of young children. I was impressed with the calm atmosphere in their home.

"Don't your children wake you up in the middle of the night?" I asked.

"Of course, they often do," I was told.

"Doesn't that cause you to become impatient with them?" I asked.

"Knowing that lack of sleep makes us vulnerable to impatience makes us try even harder. The less sleep we have, the more aware we are that we need to increase our efforts to remain patient."

That taught me what I needed to know. My belief that I had to be impatient when I lacked sleep was a self-fulfilling prophecy no longer.

LAPSES

Do not let a lapse throw you off track. You may have spent a lot of time and energy on gaining a greater amount of patience. You may have been successful many times. But then you slip and speak impatiently. Pick yourself up again and continue on the path of patience.

Some people view lapses as, "See, it's not working. I tried and tried. But I'm back to square one." This view is not accurate. Your victories are stored in your brain forever. Lapses do not erase your successes. Strengthen yourself and be resolved to increase your patience level from now on.

Expect lapses. Some people work on patience and are more patient than ever before. They tell themselves, "Now I'm so patient that I'll never be impatient again." Then, "Wham!" Something unexpected happens and throws them. Expecting lapses makes it easier for you to cope with them.

View each lapse as an opportunity to become even more patient. You will now need to make an even stronger effort. This will bolster your level of patience and increase its strength.

Since working on our character is a major reason why we are in this world, every lapse is a reminder that your mission in this world is not complete yet.

Let your own lapses in this area make you more understanding and compassionate towards others in their areas of weakness. Having your lapses accomplish this raises their value.

Understand your lapses. What are the main factors that created the impatience? Use the knowledge you have gained to prevent future lapses in these and similar situations.

I was becoming smug and complacent. I worked on character development and I was extremely patient. There was an arrogance to my thinking. I could overcome my faults. Others should be able to overcome theirs. "They are just lazy," I said to myself. "If they are sincere, they wouldn't still have their shortcomings."

Then I suffered a lapse. I said things in my impatience that I was intensely embarrassed about. The air in my arrogant balloon escaped as my balloon was punctured. This taught me an important lesson about not passing judgment on others.

REWRITE THE RERUNS

The more past memories you have of being patient, the easier it will be for you to recall them in the present. These serve as your references to enable you to be patient in the here and now.

What if you have way too many past memories of being impatient? What if your impatient memories keep popping up when you don't want them? What if you find it difficult to remember times and moments of patience?

Create patient memories for yourself. Recall situations when you were impatient. Mentally visualize yourself having reacted time and time again with absolute and total patience. Are you really allowed to do this? The answer is, "Why not?" You are not fooling anyone about how you actually reacted. But in the magnificent creative machine that is your brain, you create scene after scene of having been patient.

People who worry create imaginary scenes of what might go wrong. This is senseless and counterproductive. It is senseless because if you are going to be creative at least do it in a beneficial way. As someone who has had to work on conquering worry, I can assure you that it is so much better to create positive inner resources rather than counterproductive painful images.

Think of at least five situations in the past when you were not as patient as you would now have wished you were. Rerun those scenes seeing yourself being a super master of patience. By doing this enough times you will spontaneously react patiently in real life.

I'm a realist. The whole idea of mentally changing the past wasn't to my liking. I asked my Rabbi about this and he told me, "The Talmud states that when one repents out of love for the Creator, one's transgressions are transformed into good deeds. Why? Because with your present consciousness, good deeds are what you would have chosen. In the present you are rewriting your past history. He suggested that I utilize this tool with every single inner resource that I wished to master.